Praise for *Summoned*

Have you ever heard God whisper your name? How would you respond if He did? Megan invites you to sit down next to her and wait for your own invitation from God. She powerfully teaches you how to be still long enough to hear the gentle whisper of a Savior summoning you to His marvelous, eternal plans for your life. Through masterful word pictures and personal examples, Megan brings the Word to life in a way that anyone can grasp. But most importantly, she points you toward courageous faith. So that no matter how your future looks, you know that God's good plans for you are right around the corner and you can take that one simple step of faith. Open the pages of this study and begin the grandest adventure of your life!

Erica Wiggenhorn
Speaker and author of *Unexplainable Jesus: Rediscovering the God You Thought You Knew*

This Bible study is exactly what I've been looking for. *Summoned* explores the powerful account of Queen Esther with outstanding biblical research, powerful questions, important applications, and with a contemporary approach that makes this story important for our lives right now. Megan B. Brown is a gifted communicator in spoken and written form—and her passionate relationship with Jesus shines through every page. You'll benefit greatly if you do this study on your own or, better yet, gather a group of friends and explore this profound, insightful, and transformational study together.

Carol Kent
Executive Director of Speak Up Ministries, speaker, and author of *He Holds My Hand*

Reading, understanding, and applying biblical narratives like Esther can be difficult. With her witty and authentic personality, Megan executes the task of properly exegeting the text. By unpacking each chapter verse by verse, readers are encouraged and challenged to dig deeper into God's Word. With each word, Megan paints a picture of a big God who loves us and is able to do all things.

Justin Daniel
Pastor, Vaughn Forest Church

I've read the story of Esther countless times and conducted just as many studies of this book. *Summoned* was a refreshing new take with its depth and wit. I laughed. I marveled. Megan doesn't shy away from hard topics, but she does so with simplicity, clarity, cultural insight, and biblical truth.

Michelle Ami Reyes
Vice President of the Asian American Christian Collaborative, Co-Executive Director of Pax, and author of *Becoming All Things*

Megan Brown is a woman on a mission to build the kingdom of God. Her contagious enthusiasm for God's Word has personally challenged me to dig deeper into the treasures of Scripture and now she invites you to do the same. Within the pages of *Summoned* is an invaluable gift—the opportunity to dive into the Word alongside this woman of God and be inspired by her passion for Christ and dedication to truth. Let her passion become yours as you journey together through the story of Esther and uncover new truths about a woman in Scripture both broken and bold and about the God who redeems all our brokenness for His glory.

Sara Barratt
Author of *Love Riot: A Teenage Call to Live with Relentless Abandon for Christ*

We can either walk out this life doing things our way or we can walk it out doing things God's way. God's way is always the best, but sometimes we have trouble surrendering our agenda and our ideas in exchange for His plan and His better way. If you're ready to do things God's way and you want to know how to walk that out, this book is for you.

Jill Savage
Author of *Real Moms . . . Real Jesus: Meet the Friend Who Understands*

If you are looking for a Bible study to make you dig in and learn about a book of the Bible in a new, fresh, deep-dive way, RUN and grab your copy of *Summoned*. I found this study challenging, encouraging, and an awakening to ask God what impossible He wanted to do through me. Megan writes as a trusted, transparent, and humorous guide who takes us straight to the Bible to dive deep into the life-changing words in the book of Esther. I left the pages of this Bible study wanting to answer God's call to watch Him use me to do the impossible.

Jennifer Hand
Executive Director of Coming Alive Ministries

Are you a woman who is seeking to fulfill her purpose for life and kingdom work? Then Megan Brown's new Bible study, *Summoned*, is a perfect beckoning to a life of radical adventure alongside the King of kings! I love to dig deep into God's Word, mining the original biblical language for nuance and strength. Make no mistake about it, this is not your typical exploration of Queen Esther's story, but a radical call for women to arise and conquer, all in God's name and for His glory. Brown has done the work and invited us to join her in the battle—all you have to do is respond to the summons to be a world changer, armed with truth and power.

Lucinda Secrest McDowell
Award-winning author of *Soul Strong* and *Life-Giving Choices*

AN 8-WEEK STUDY OF *Esther*

Answering a Call

to the Impossible

SUMMONED

MEGAN B. BROWN

MOODY PUBLISHERS

CHICAGO

Scripture quotations, unless otherwise noted, are taken from the ESV® Bible (The Holy Bible, English Standard Version®), copyright © 2001 by Crossway, a publishing ministry of Good News Publishers. Used by permission. All rights reserved.

Scripture quotations marked (NIV) are taken from the Holy Bible, New International Version®, NIV®. Copyright © 1973, 1978, 1984, 2011 by Biblica, Inc.™ Used by permission of Zondervan. All rights reserved worldwide. www.zondervan.com The "NIV" and "New International Version" are trademarks registered in the United States Patent and Trademark Office by Biblica, Inc.™

All emphasis in Scripture has been added.

Published in association with the literary agency of The Steve Laube Agency, 24 W. Camelback Road, A-635, Phoenix, AZ 85013.

Edited by Pamela Joy Pugh
Interior design: Kaylee Lockenour
Cover design: Faceout Studio
Cover illustration of silhouette copyright © 2019 by TairA / Sutterstock (308020865). All rights reserved.
Author photo: Andi Adams

Library of Congress Cataloging-in-Publication Data

Names: Brown, Megan B., author.
Title: Summoned : answering a call to the impossible / Megan B. Brown.
Description: Chicago : Moody Publishers, [2021] | Includes bibliographical
  references. | Summary: "In Summoned, you'll enter the story of
  Esther-her calling, pain, and role in God's plan for salvation-and see
  how God is always working in the lives of His people, even when He seems
  distant. Through this 8-week study, you'll develop a deeper appreciation
  for God's Word and begin to see that stepping out in faith for His glory
  is often the first step to encountering His redeeming love"-- Provided
  by publisher.
Identifiers: LCCN 2020050476 (print) | LCCN 2020050477 (ebook) | ISBN
  9780802421692 (paperback) | ISBN 9780802499295 (ebook)
Subjects: LCSH: Bible. Esther--Textbooks.
Classification: LCC BS1375.55 .B76 2021 (print) | LCC BS1375.55 (ebook) |
  DDC 222/.906--dc23
LC record available at https://lccn.loc.gov/2020050476
LC ebook record available at https://lccn.loc.gov/2020050477

Originally delivered by fleets of horse-drawn wagons, the affordable paperbacks from D. L. Moody's publishing house resourced the church and served everyday people. Now, after more than 125 years of publishing and ministry, Moody Publishers' mission remains the same—even if our delivery systems have changed a bit. For more information on other books (and resources) created from a biblical perspective, go to www.moodypublishers.com or write to:

Moody Publishers
820 N. LaSalle Boulevard
Chicago, IL 60610

1 3 5 7 9 10 8 6 4 2

Printed in the United States of America

DEDICATION

In memory of Galen Norsworthy.

To my husband, Keith, who has paved the road that I run upon. Thank you for your unending support, your sacrifices, and your partnership in serving Jesus.

To my pastors, Dr. Blake Henderson and Justin Daniel: Benefiting from your leadership has been one of the utmost privileges of my life, and I am beyond grateful for every word of instruction and encouragement.

To my Mama: Your belief in me has spurred me forward, shaped me, and made me strong.

To the Unicorn Tribe: Katie, Catherine, Terry, Laura, Andi, and Jess. As a military spouse, I couldn't have asked for anything more than the immense love all of you have shown me.

To my friend Erica Wiggenhorn. You unlocked the door for me, my friend, and I haven't looked back.

And finally, to the beautiful staff persons at the D'Iberville and Warner Robins Chick-fil-A. Chicken nuggets were essential in the writing of this book.

CONTENTS

FOREWORD

For the word of God is living and active, sharper than any two-edged sword, piercing to the division of soul and of spirit, of joints and marrow, and discerning the thoughts and intentions of the heart. —Hebrews 4:12

The next several weeks may very well change the trajectory of your life. You are in for a challenge and you are in for a treat. The book of Esther has long been a favorite of mine. Many of you may be familiar with Esther's story from hearing about it in Sunday school as a young child. *Summoned* is not a Sunday school version of this Old Testament book. For those of you brand new to Bible study, you are in very capable hands as you read the words penned here by Megan Brown.

I first met Megan backstage at a women's leadership conference. I was immediately taken by her bright-colored hair, which matched her edgy and vibrant personality. But what stayed with me was the intensity and sincerity in her eyes as she shared about her passion for equipping women and especially her commitment to discipling military spouses and building into the military community. Equal to her love and loyalty to her family and community is her love for God's Word.

I've invested the last three decades plus in vocational Christian ministry, and what I've observed across the country is a steady decline in biblical literacy. Often Bible reading or devotional time is reduced to reading a single verse with a few paragraphs written about the one verse in mostly story form by a Christian writer. Without cultural background, context of the passage, and an understanding of the history of the time, it is easy for us to misread and misunderstand the original intent and meaning of the single verse. Often, especially in North America, we take on a very "me-centered" approach when reading the Bible. We treat the Bible like a horoscope or fortune cookie, looking for a message for ourselves, and miss the actual purpose of reading God's Word—insight and knowledge of God Himself for the purpose of growing in our intimacy and love *for Him.*

What Megan offers in *Summoned* is a comprehensive approach to help the learner become more confident in the area of Bible study and in that way become a self-feeder. Not only does the reader study an entire book of the Bible verse by verse, but included throughout the chapters are practical tools and Bible study methods. These principles and tips are both practical and sound approaches to the study of God's Word. Your ability to mine God's Word for the treasure of knowledge of God, His will, His ways, and His heart will absolutely transform your day-to-day life.

In addition to a robust offering of the how-to's of Bible study, Megan also addresses very real and painful realities of the challenges not only facing the people during Esther's time but also what we currently face in our world today. Esther is not a Disney fairy tale, and I'm grateful Megan doesn't gloss over the harder parts of the story.

The God who made the world and all things in it, the One who knows each star by name and the number of hairs on our head, has made a way through His Son and through His Word for us to intimately know Him. The possibilities are endless of the ways God will lead, direct, provide, comfort, and strengthen each of you as you invest these weeks and beyond to the faithful study of God's Word.

VIVIAN MABUNI
Speaker, Podcast Host, and Author of *Open Hands, Willing Heart*

WELCOME

Dearest One,

I want to thank you for beginning this journey with me. I don't know the obstacles or hindrances that you may have faced to come to this place, but I'm glad you're here. You may be wondering what to expect, especially if this is your first Bible study.

Several years ago, I was given my first Bible study by a close friend. She gifted me a copy of Erica Wiggenhorn's *Ezekiel: Every Life Positioned for Purpose*. I have to admit that I was a little intimidated by the amount of reading and homework. A few of my friends and I were going to walk through this together, so the task seemed less daunting.

I had never completed a workbook-style Bible study, but I was eager to learn. Through the daily discipline of engaging with the Scriptures, the encouragement from my friends, and the dogged determination of our home church to present the real Jesus found within God's Word, my heart was filled with His truths. Together, they unlocked the door for me to understanding God's Word and His sovereign will.

I want to give that gift to you. I want to help break down the barriers that stand between you and His truth.

Over the next eight weeks, we are going to explore the book of Esther. (Week Eight, "Summoned to Serve," will be one session rather than five, and will give you a chance to wrap up and respond to what we have learned together.) We are going to excavate God's truths by observing the characters involved, analyzing the culture, and filtering our findings through what we discover in the New Testament.

God speaks through story. God teaches us about Himself by telling us the story of His people, where they lived, and what they did.

This book of the Bible is about a woman who found herself in danger and doubt. She lived in a culture where God was not a priority and where He was not worshiped. We are about to see what happens when God moves through circumstances and hardship, albeit in an unseen manner.

We are going to learn that He still moves today.

When you and I begin to understand that God is faithful, no matter our circumstances, we can begin to walk boldly in obedience and love. I fundamentally believe that we cannot love whom we do not know. My greatest hope is that at the end of our eight weeks together, you will see how God is faithful, even when it feels like He is nowhere to be found.

MY STORY

Have you ever felt overwhelmed at the thought of studying the Bible?

It's funny how we can begin to panic or feel defeated by such a gift. God has given us His Word so that we can know Him, understand His will, and ultimately to tell us the story of His redeeming grace in Jesus. Unfortunately, often this gift feels more like an obligation. "Read the Bible" is added to the long list of our to-dos.

Many years ago, I was gifted a Bible. It was an NIV (New International Version) and had my name embossed on the front of its brown leather cover. The pages were lined with gold foil and had a lot of words printed in red. The pages were tissue thin and the names of the individual books were tabbed and indexed. To me, it was the scariest book in the world.

I had no context for reading it. In a frenzied fit to try to approach the task of hearing God, I decided that I would read it from one cover to the other (ambitious, I know). I started in Genesis and, once I got to an amazingly long list of names, I gave up. I felt defeated and stupid. I bought the lie, the lie straight from hell, that this book was not for me. Maybe you're in the midst of that lie today. Perhaps reading the Bible has been a point of pain or has been frustrating for you. Today, I hope that changes. As we unpack the homework together, I pray that you are encouraged. You can do this!

Several years would pass before I felt brave enough to venture back into the Bible's pages. But today I invite you to jump into this story with me. I want to serve as a conversation partner as you step courageously toward the task of Bible study. So, as we hit the play button and start this story, grab a cup of coffee (tea, if that is your jam) and let's go together.

There was a time when I was complacent in my minimal Bible reading, but a season swiftly approached that would shake me to my very core. This season sped toward me with the intensity of a head-on collision and this "car crash" wrecked my world.

My husband is active duty military and, many years ago, we had to face a deployment followed by an immediate PCS (permanent change of station, or military move). He was deployed to the Middle East for over six months, leaving me with our three children who, at the time, were five, three, and one. Add in the fact that we were stationed remotely (an hour away from the nearest military installation) and that I had a crippling case of postpartum depression, I had a real situation on my hands.

Needless to say, we were in for quite a rough time. This deployment challenged me and showed me my great need for God, who could walk with me through that very present hardship.

Has there ever been a season where you desperately needed God to show up?

About halfway through the deployment, a postal worker rang my doorbell. "Good morning, ma'am. Could you please open your garage so that I can deliver these footlockers? Looks like someone is coming home, huh?" I froze. I hadn't heard from my husband in weeks. He wasn't due home for another three months. I fell to my knees and began to sob.

I'm pretty sure that I scared the daylights out of this poor postal worker. She unloaded the footlockers into my garage and I just sat on my couch, blankly staring at the wall.

Terrible thoughts started to race through my mind. Worry consumed me. One sentence seemed to be on loop, as if it was being shouted through a megaphone, and drowned out the sound of everything else. "My husband is dead and I am all alone." Peace was nowhere to be found.

In a moment of clarity, the Holy Spirit prompted me to pick up my Bible. I opened it to 1 Thessalonians and just began reading. I read the whole book. None of it made sense to me and I couldn't figure out its message. "Pray without ceasing" was the only thing that I could grasp. *Okay,* I thought. I continued to faithfully flip through the pages, hoping to understand. Peace began to wash over me, and I was able to rest. This was the day I decided I needed to know how to read my Bible. I had to know what this book said and why.

Several days would pass until I would hear from my husband. As it turned out, Keith was moving from one of the smaller bases overseas to a larger location, and he had shipped his footlockers home without telling me. Believe me, that poor man got an earful for scaring me nearly to death.

When the phone finally rang and I heard the beautiful sound of my husband's voice, I was beyond grateful for two things. First, I praised God that Keith was safe. Second, I was grateful that in a moment of one of my greatest fears, God crashed in on me and gave me peace through His Word.

I want to encourage you today.

The Bible is most certainly for you, and for you *right now*. You may not be in the throes of a deployment, but I would be willing to bet that there are some very present obstacles you are facing. In the middle of messy and difficult lives, God is patiently and gently calling you to walk with Him. He has given you His Word as a way to know Him, love Him, and serve Him in Jesus.

Now my days are spent lavishly feasting in the love of God's Word. I can't say that things are always perfect. Being a military spouse is tough, and many days, I find myself longing for stability. But, knowing that God has ordained every set of orders and every relocation, I can honestly say that it is well.

I pray that it is well with you too.

MAKING THE MOST OF THIS STUDY

First, take a deep breath. You can do this.

Second, one of the best things you can do is to invite another along for the journey. An African proverb I hold close to my heart says, "If you want to go fast, go alone. If you want to go far, go together." My advice is to "go together." Grab a friend or a neighbor and ask her to join you. Or, if you have a few friends who want to learn more about who God is, take this trip as a small group.

By the end of this workbook, you will have read all ten chapters of the book of Esther. The daily homework covers a specific section of the text and will have response questions to help you piece together the plot and meaning. There will also be questions that will help prompt you to ponder your circumstances, yourself, and ultimately, your Father in heaven.

Make sure to read the assigned passage in its entirety. Also, many apps and websites have an audio Bible feature. I love to use this feature at Biblegateway.com. The Scriptures quoted throughout this book are from the English Standard Version, unless otherwise noted. But feel free to use any version that you are comfortable with.

If you are facilitating this study for a small group, a leader's guide can be found at www.meganbbrown.com, along with additional resources.

Here are a few additional suggestions to make your study time more effective.

Praise: I like to begin my own study time by putting on one of my favorite worship songs and creating an atmosphere of worship. Create a playlist of your favorites and spend some time in praise. Give God the worship He deserves.

Pray: I allow myself to focus on the Lord and pray that He will enable my heart to be still. I ask Him for the discipline to stay the course and wisdom to understand His truth. Say or write out your prayers to God. Let Him hear your heart for Him.

Pursue: Go deeper into the text. Ask questions and make notes. I am a "book-writer-inner" (I'm not even sure if that is a word). I write in and through the margins and free spaces of books. I dog-ear, doodle, scribble prayers, and make notes. Honestly, nothing would make me happier than to meet you face to face one day with a copy of this book and see its pages covered in ink.

I wish we were sitting across from each other and sharing our stories over coffee. I would tell you how excited I am to walk through the Scriptures with you and that I couldn't wait to hear about what you are learning. Being obedient in listening to God through searching His Word is a noble undertaking, and I pray you will be truly blessed with wisdom and encouragement along the way.

BUT FIRST, THE GOOD NEWS

The gospel of Jesus Christ is clearly evident through the pages of Scripture. In fact, every single Scripture is either leading up to, or a result of, the gospel. Everything in the Bible, from cover to cover, is about God and His plan to redeem His creation through Christ Jesus.

What does that mean for you and me?

It means we have been given a gift. We have been saved by faith, through grace, *and* have been given a way to know our Father in heaven through His Word.

It means we have an unshakable hope.

The brokenness we experience here on earth is not the end, and it does not get the final say—God does. And because Christ willingly laid down His life two thousand years ago and took it up again, we have been made new. We are now co-heirs with Jesus. We are redeemed.

Through studying Esther in light of the gospel, we will be able to pull out some amazing truths. But we can't do that without a full and robust understanding of the gospel. Many times when we think of "the gospel," religious tracts or sales pitches come to mind. Sharing this central truth of the Christian faith is not a "conversion conversation" or a cheesy social media meme. It is a truth that rings to the deepest levels of our very soul.

But what is the gospel?

Let me paint you a picture.

The Greek word for "gospel" in the New Testament is the Greek word *euangelion.* This word was originally a military term.

In biblical times, when Israel was battling against a warring nation, it was customary for a messenger, or town crier of sorts, to run ahead of the incoming soldiers to declare the outcome of battle. If Israel was on the losing side, bad things were coming. Men would be killed in the streets. Women and children could be raped, sold into slavery, or killed. It was a terrifying thing. If Israel lost, death and bondage would be marching on them.

On the other hand, if Israel prevailed, the town crier would run through the streets, screaming "*victory!*" Victory. "Victory! Freedom! God has been our help and delivered us!" The word "*euangelion!*" is the Greek translation of the Hebrew word for victory. I love that this is the word the New Testament writers chose to deliver the "good news" of Jesus Christ.

We have that same victory in Jesus today. In Him, we are free from the bonds of slavery to sin or death. We have been reconciled with God—made right with Him, through the cross of Christ.

This is the gospel.

When God created the world, His intention was to spend eternity in fellowship with us. We were created to love, obey, and worship God. His heart was for us to walk with Him for all of our lives.

When sin entered the world through disobedience, we were separated from God and there was nothing we could do to restore ourselves on our own. There was no deed, no list of actions, and no amount of being a "good and biblical woman" that could bring us back.

God, in His abounding love, gave Jesus, His one and only Son, as a sacrifice to atone for our sins.

Sin is our denial of God's character and our failure to abide within God's laws. The hard truth is that we are completely incapable of living by the letter of the law of God, nor are we able to always accept who God says He is. We fail and falter. We sin, again and again.

Romans 6 tells us that "the wages of sin is death." But God, through Christ, has made a way for us to be made right with Him.

Only through Christ are we redeemed and reconciled with God. Our sins are no longer counted, and forgiveness abounds from the throne of grace because of Christ's perfect life, sacrificial death, and miraculous resurrection from the dead. When He rose from the dead, in His physical body, He conquered sin and death.

We can walk in newness of life, free from the shame and guilt of our past, our choices, or our failures. We can now hope in life eternally spent with Him, proven and made possible by the powerful death and resurrection of Christ.

This, friends, is *good news*.

We can, with reckless abandon, leave our past and the pain of our choices on the altar. We can lay them down, knowing that they do not determine our worth, or our value, to our Father in heaven. They are not our identity. Our identity rests with Him, as the daughters of the King Most High.

When we accept that we are sinners and that Jesus is the Son of God, able to take the penalty for our sin, we are then viewed by God through Jesus' righteousness and not our own. Jesus paid it all, the penalty for sin, for us.

If someone dragged you into doing this study with them, I hope you feel overwhelmed by love. And if they invited you in for the sake of Christ, that you may know Him and love Him more deeply, I want to talk to you.

Today can be the day. Today can be the day when you get to lay down all the hurt, shame, and hate for the hard things this life has given you. Today you can approach God through belief in His Son, Jesus, and walk in newness of life—one full of the hope we have in Christ.

As Christians, we believe that entering into a relationship with God starts here, and in no other way: with faith in Jesus.

Once you believe that Jesus is the Son of God and He died for your sins, share it with someone. Tell the person who gave you this book. Tell a pastor. Tell anyone! While the angels rejoice in heaven, let God's family rejoice with you here on earth.

Let's Get Started

Brokenness is everywhere, and it has touched everything. Today, we as women can often feel lost and overwhelmed in our seasons of waiting or in times of longing. We remain chained to the past or to poor choices. These circumstances should not render us inactive, but so many times, we have lost the courage to move in the face of obstacles or opposition. It is time for us to reclaim our identity in the God of heaven and walk in faith with Him by studying His Word, specifically now the book of Esther.

This book in the Bible is a story about a Jewish woman named Hadassah, later called Esther, who lived in Persia after the Babylonian exile from Jerusalem. She lived among those who did not return to Jerusalem under Zerubbabel, and her story is filled with hardship, hurt, and heinous events. As a woman, Esther had to endure long-suffering and uncertainty. She made difficult choices and was forced into a lifestyle where faith was not favored. God's people were living outside of His promised land, exiled from their holy city, and presumably from His presence. An edict was issued that subjected countless women to sexual abuse and degradation.

This study will not be an exercise recounting the children's version of Esther, with beauty pageants and pretty tiaras. *Summoned: Answering a Call to the Impossible* is a rough and raw look at the biblical text. Cultural Christianity, a shallow and self-centered view of God and the world, has watered God's Word down to a suggested blueprint for living, filled with short quips and encouraging phrases. This assumption couldn't be further from the truth. We will reject the notion that God's Word is only for the purposes of self-discovery or finding validation for our own religiosity. Instead, we open the pages of our Bibles expecting to hear truths about hard topics, causing us to grapple with God. These are the truths that will forever shatter chains we have been unable to break.

How can a book of the Bible with no mention of God at all teach us about our world today, much less teach us about Him? It is within the story of one woman that we become familiar with the unseen God. In fact—spoiler alert—this story isn't about Esther at all. It's about God and how He moves, in spite of unbelief, disobedience, or pain.

Through the rise and fall of queens, the racist and harsh schemes of hateful men, and the victory only God can give, our study of the life of Esther will bring us to the place where we can truly say that "we know that for those who love God all things work together for good, for those who are called according to his purpose" (Romans 8:28).

There has been much teaching of late that makes boastful promises of health and wealth when one becomes or remains a believer in Jesus Christ. The ripples of this false teaching have washed over an entire generation of believers and into a culture that rejects God altogether.

How can the church respond, when the church and cultural Christianity are responsible for many of these poor doctrines and heretical messages? It is time for the church to rise anew and walk boldly in the calling to believe rightly by ardently studying and proclaiming what God's Word actually says.

The yield of this filtered and filigreed pseudo gospel has been faithless fruit. Women have been led astray, blown in the wind by every new doctrine. Faith has been shallow and empty-handed in times of trial. Worst of all, the gospel that women have so desperately needed has been replaced with a self-care–centered approach to experiencing God.

But this is what we are here to do: to study the Bible with the intent of understanding *rightly*, through culture and context. All of this is for the goal of *rightly* comprehending so that we can live out what we *rightly* believe.

The truth is this: our God is faithful; He never leaves or forsakes; His love is shown in His promises, namely in His Son Jesus' sacrificial death, burial, and resurrection, and not in His provision of a comfortable or pleasing life.

In the dark and desolate places of this life, at the side of deathbeds and destroyed hope, God is there with us. These hardships are inevitable and part of a life away from heaven. These things too will pass away, but the Word of the Lord endures forever.

We can rest in this truth: no matter what this life may bring, God loves His people and He is faithful. You and I can stand firm in the understanding that, even though His actions are sometimes unseen, God is constantly working in the lives of His beloved children.

Ask yourself a few questions:

Do I believe that God's Word should direct my steps?

Do I want to hear what He says about how we should live our lives?

Do I believe that my individual faith walk could have immeasurable kingdom impact?

If you answered yes, we can begin the task of seeking God together. We can dive into the depths of His Word, expecting Him to speak to us.

God's Word is given to us that we may know Him and love Him deeply. He reveals Himself to us in the ardent study of His Word—in the discipline of coming to Him, expectant to hear what He has to say.

As a result, we can begin, through the power of the Holy Spirit, to transform our lives. We begin to walk with God, in love and righteousness. We can rest in His truth, through times of peace or in turmoil, knowing that He is sovereign.

Finally, through immersing ourselves in His Word—the story of God's redemption of humanity through the finished work of Jesus—we can learn how to love God, follow Jesus, and live our lives for His glory.

Summoned is a resounding call for us to return to God, to turn away from "cultural Christianity," to walk in our identity in Christ through faith and, in light of the finished work of the cross, to wholly commit ourselves to the mission and purpose of Jesus: to become disciples and to make them, which is the Great Commission.

SUMMONED

to the Start

WEEK 1 | DAY 1

READ ESTHER CHAPTER 1.

SCRIPTURE FOCUS: Esther 1:1–4

We begin this story, which spans the course of ten years, in the city of Susa, the citadel, where Ahasuerus sat on the throne. Susa's locale would be in modern-day Iran. Susa, or the Hebrew name, Shushan, was one of four capital cities of the Persian Empire; the other three were Babylon, Ecbatana, and Persepolis. Here we see that events in the Bible happened in real time and on the map. These are not simply bedtime stories or fairy tales we teach our children to elicit good behavior. The beginning of this story does not start with "Once upon a time, in a land far, far away."

Instead, Esther 1:1 begins with:

"_____, the Ahasuerus who reigned from India to Ethiopia over 127 provinces . . ."

The phrase "now in the days of" indicates that this passage should be understood as history.

In other words, "This is what happened."

We are going to dig deeper into methods of better Bible study together. When we read the Bible, we have to know that there is no other book like it. The Bible contains a vast array of genres, or categories—everything from poetry to prophecy, history to letters, gospel accounts to parables can be found within its pages. Approaching the Scriptures calls for us to ask some questions about the nature of what we are reading. Reading the Bible requires us to learn the skill of interpretation so that we can rightly practice what we believe. It is vital to understand how we should interpret each genre used in Scripture because, **if we don't, we run the risk of missing God.**

One of the goals for the next eight weeks together is to spend time developing a habit of daily Bible study, using and practicing interpretation skills. As we journey through the book of Esther, line by line and verse by verse, we will begin to ask questions of the text. The answers to these questions will help us interpret what the Scriptures are trying to teach us.

WHY DO YOU THINK IT IS IMPORTANT FOR US TO KNOW IF THE SCRIPTURE WE ARE READING IS HISTORY OR POETRY OR SOMETHING ELSE? DOES IT MAKE A DIFFERENCE IN HOW WE UNDERSTAND OR APPLY WHAT WE HAVE READ?

When I became a believer, I wasn't familiar with the Bible. Even after I accepted Christ, I had no idea how to read it, much less study it. I would flop my Bible open on my desk and ask God "What are You trying to tell me?" For the record, this is *not* a great Bible study method. Building our beliefs or behaviors on "one-liners" of text or Bible verses taken out of context is one of the worst things we can do when seeking God.

I truly believed that there was no possible way that I could understand it. *It's not for me,* I would tell myself. *I need to wait until Sunday, when someone more qualified can explain it.* I would grab my Bible on the way to our Sunday church service. When we arrived home, I would put it right back on the shelf where it would stay until the next Sunday morning.

WHAT ARE YOUR STRUGGLES WHEN IT COMES TO SITTING DOWN AND
STUDYING YOUR BIBLE?

FIND 2 TIMOTHY 3:16–17. COPY THE VERSES BELOW.

All scripture is God-breathed & is useful for teaching, rebuking, correcting & training in righteousness, so that the servant of God may be equipped for every good work.

Scripture is "breathed out by God" and "profitable" for us. But more than that, this Scripture tells us that we are incomplete without it. God is teaching us that we cannot be fully finished, fully equipped, without His Word. The Greek word used for the phrase "having been fully equipped" is *exartizó*.[1] It paints a picture of us being finished and "completed" by our interaction with God's Word. These verses illuminate the truth of our great need for Him in our lives and His invitation to go deeper into relationship through the ardent study of the Bible.

Let's dive into the text and talk about Ahasuerus for a minute. "Ahasuerus" is the Hebrew translation for the Persian name "Khshayarshan" (try saying that three times fast). Your translation may use the name "Xerxes," which is the Greek translation of his Persian name. All in all, it is the same guy.

We are also given geographical information about where and when King Ahasuerus reigned. He reigned from India to Ethiopia, and historically, he ruled from 485 to 465 BC.[2]

The passage also tells us who was present for an epic party.

WHO ATTENDED THE BANQUET IN THE KING'S PALACE (ESTHER 1:3)?

This was quite a crowd!

The Scriptures do not give us a reason for this gathering, but the ancient secular historian Herodotus may be able to shed some light on this gathering. In his *History*, he records that Ahasuerus was calling together a war council in order to plan an invasion of Greece. Ahasuerus's father invaded Greece and was sorely defeated. Herodotus suggests that Ahasuerus planned to "reduce the whole earth into one empire."[3] Ambitious dude, right?

HOW LONG DID THIS BANQUET LAST (V. 4)?

So Ahasuerus is planning to march the war path and brings all his nobles and officials together. As we read, he was hosting these officials for 180 days. That sounds like quite the social occasion! But keeping in mind the distances involved and the time needed for traveling—plus traveling with their own entourages of servants—six months doesn't sound unrealistic. In addition, he may have been entertaining in shifts for those six months rather than taking too many people away from their needed positions for too long of a time.

This is the context for the book of Esther. Everything we learn from this point on will be built on this beginning.

We have a king who is planning for war, is very prideful, and seeks to conquer the world. The Scripture says that "he showed the riches of his royal glory and the splendor and pomp of his greatness" (Esther 1:4).

The entire first chapter is about the king. God is not mentioned once, nor is He mentioned at all throughout the entire book of Esther. (Don't worry, we will certainly come back to this.) However, in this passage, the king is mentioned six times. The writer of the book is introducing us to an empire that is wholly focused on the king, not God. All aspects of life for the characters in this story are centralized around the whims and whining of a king, not *the* King.

As we continue this journey through Esther, we will see that God works within and through the lives of many individuals, whether they acknowledge Him as Lord or not. And we will watch as these characters plot and scheme, supposedly controlling their circumstances. The book of Esther is going to show us that God is most certainly sovereign and that He is faithful.

Take a moment to jot down a prayer for our time together. Ask God to give you a desire for His Word. Maybe ask Him for the discipline to rise to the task. Tell Him about what you think will hold you back or get in the way of your time in Scripture. As you compile your thoughts, I pray that you will begin to trust Him to carry you through the next eight weeks.

WEEK 1 | DAY 2

READ ESTHER CHAPTER 1.

SCRIPTURE FOCUS: Esther 1:5–9

We pick up from yesterday, after a six-month long shindig, to the beginning of a feast that lasts for seven days.

Does anyone remember *MTV Cribs*? A camera crew would get invited into some of the most grandiose homes owned by celebrities. These people then would give an all-access tour of their homes, allowing us—the poor and unfortunate viewer—to see the glamour of the celebrity lifestyle.

The sheer excess was almost overwhelming. The absurd collections of cars, the guest houses, and the opulence was the showcase of the docuseries. Some of these people have closets with more square footage than my entire house.

This is the kind of excess that the people of Susa would have been met with.

The ornate setting and abundant wealth of the king was displayed to such a degree that even the drinkware was deemed notable by Esther's author. "Drinks were served in golden vessels, vessels of different kinds" (Esther 1:7).

WHO ATTENDED THIS BANQUET (ESTHER 1:5)?

"All the people . . . both great and small" would include the Jewish people. Here is a vast empire, an empire of the rich and elite, that would not usually include "both great and small." Nevertheless, the Jewish people find themselves in the midst of this elaborate and abundant feast.

WHERE DID THIS FEAST TAKE PLACE (V. 5)?

Let's note something interesting about the location of this next banquet. The word "garden" in Arabic is translated as "paradise." The Arabic meaning would be a beautiful and lush area with flowing water . . . in the desert. Reread verse 6 for a picture of the greatness of this palace.

The court of the garden of the king's palace is also an allusion to the temple in Jerusalem.

Another place is described with as much detail: Solomon's temple.

The original audience would have understood this attention to detail and would have grasped that this reference evokes the holy city of Jerusalem. When we begin to read through the passages of Scripture, we need to notice changes in rhythms, repetitive words, and details. We also need to ask questions of the text.

I want to give you a mini crash course in *hermeneutics*, which is simply the art and science of Bible study. The art of Bible study is found in us. Some of us doodle, journal, or even draw through the Scriptures to gain understanding. Methods of personal interpretation can vary, but the science of Bible study is in the formulas and procedures of breaking down the text.

So, with today's homework as the example text, let's walk through unpacking the book of Esther using some principles of hermeneutics.

Ask questions. Find meaning. Bridge the gap.

Here are a few of the questions to ask and answer when studying God's Word.

Who wrote this book?

Why was it written?

Who was it written for?

What would they have understood it to mean?

How does the original meaning translate to me today?

The original audience of our text was the Jewish people. They would be familiar with "The Book of the Law," called the Torah, or, as we know it, the first five books of the Old Testament, which were written by Moses. They would have been familiar with their history and the temple.

TURN TO 1 KINGS, CHAPTERS 6 AND 7, AND GIVE IT A SKIM. HOW IS THE TEMPLE DESCRIBED?

The construction of the temple and its furnishings are recorded in painstaking detail. This was to be the place that God was worshiped by His people. But here, in Esther 1, in the king's inner court, the people are there to worship the god of Persia, King Ahasuerus.

READ EZRA 6:5. WHAT WAS TAKEN FROM GOD'S HOUSE (THE TEMPLE) AND BROUGHT TO BABYLON BY NEBUCHADNEZZAR WHEN JERUSALEM WAS OVERTAKEN?

Could it be, in the midst of all of this apparent paradise, that there is a painful reminder of what was lost? (You might remember from history class that Babylon was conquered by Persia.)

The very golden cups that were consecrated and made separate for service to the Lord were being used for pagan drinking parties. It is almost as if this note by the author adds insult to injury. Ahasuerus is parading around as if he is a god, and part of his obnoxious wealth includes treasures once held by God's people.

This passage begins the usage and patterns of irony.

Irony is a literary tool that we will see used throughout this entire book. (Cue Alanis Morissette . . .) All throughout the book of Esther will be situations that seem like mere coincidence and many circumstances that are drastic role reversals.

Being able to identify the rhythmic patterns and changes will help us navigate through building our beliefs and practicing them with a proper understanding. I may be hitting this interpretation thing pretty hard, but the proper interpretation of the Bible is vital for us. **Our ability to grasp God's Word will shape how we see Him, how we see others, and, ultimately, how we live our lives.**

As we continue to unpack these verses, we cling to the truth that everything recorded in Scripture is important. Every list of names, plots of land allotments, and seemingly unimportant details are essential and rich in meaning.

WHAT WAS THE EDICT ISSUED BY THE KING IN VERSE 8?

This tells us something about Persia; it is a place that is governed by laws. That could be good news, right? This must mean that there are ruling bodies and systems of justice. For the Jews, a people living outside their promised land as foreigners, it might mean due process and protocol, fairness, and an expectation of continuity. Maybe even, they could trust in the safety of the land.

However, the king made a decree that stated there would be "no compulsion" for drinking. That's concerning. King Ahasuerus has just declared a six-month long Mardi Gras and regulated that each man plays "flip cup" until he is satisfied. Sounds like a place where good and godly decisions are made, right? Not so much.

Let's take Esther 1:8, for example, and filter it through one of cultural Christianity's favorite habits. Let's put it on a coffee cup or super cute journal (taken completely out of context and divorced from its actual meaning) and use it as a systematic pillar of belief.

Can't you just see it? I'm picturing a very fashionable woman, with long and flowing curls. She's wearing a trendy hat, leather feather earrings, and is sporting a wine glass with "There is no compulsion, Esther 1:8" etched in scripted font. Cute. That sounds like biblically sanctioned drunkenness.

This is why we have to do the work of seriously developing strong Bible study skills. If we don't do it, we run the risk of misapplying the text because we impose meaning that is not there. In the Instagram filtered and flowered land of cultural Christianity, we find that the Bible is cut into pleasing snippets and bumper-sticker phrases that we can simply slap over hard circumstances like a Band-Aid. They carry little meaning and leave much to be desired.

In order to combat the mistake of superimposing meaning onto a text, we have to *exegete* the Scriptures. Exegesis is the critical interpretation of the biblical text to discover its *intended* meaning. Exegesis is the process of reading the text and analyzing it to uncover what it means. We do this with the goal in mind of understanding the principle in the passage. We have to understand what the text is actually saying in order to apply it to our everyday lives.

Let's go back to the text. The king had "given orders to all the staff of his palace to do as each man desired" (Esther 1:8).

We see that Persia indeed had laws, but what happens when these laws are absurd and nonsensical? Diving further into the book of Esther, we will see these laws in action and reflect on the ripple effect these laws dictate. An edict about drinking "with no compulsion" is a little scary and another indicator of this king's character.

In verse 9, we are introduced to Vashti, the king's queen. This addition almost feels like an afterthought. Here are all sorts of great things about this guy who owns all this stuff and throws great parties . . . "Oh, yeah." There is this queen who threw a party too.

When I read this line, I imagine the author listing out all Ahasuerus's wealth and splendor. Then the author includes his final prized possession, a woman. Vashti is just another shiny object belonging to the king, a thing to be desired and exploited.

BASED ON WHAT WE'VE READ SO FAR, HOW WOULD YOU DESCRIBE KING AHASUERUS?

As we continue through this journey together, I want to share a study method that has been widely used; pastor and Bible teacher David Platt has been credited with its development. It is called the REAP method. **Read. Examine. Apply. Pray.** This is just one of many tools that you can use to grow in a deeper understanding of God's Word. Try it here.

Read Esther 1.

WHAT ARE SOME THINGS THAT JUMP OUT AT YOU?

ARE THERE ANY DETAILS THAT REQUIRE A DEEPER LOOK FOR YOU TO EXAMINE?

WHAT ARE SOME POSSIBLE APPLICATIONS FROM THE TEXT?

HOW CAN YOU PRAY OVER THIS SECTION OF SCRIPTURE?

WEEK 1 | DAY 3

READ ESTHER CHAPTER 1.

SCRIPTURE FOCUS: Esther 1:10–15

Big trucks. This may be a southern thing, but have you ever seen a young man driving down the road in an excessively massive truck? These trucks usually have a lift kit and roll bars, and they might even be "duallies" (for y'all who aren't sure what this means, it denotes dual tires on the rear axle). These excessive trucks usually incite some sort of joke about the confidence, or overcompensation, of the driver.

While I do not believe that *all* big truck drivers are overcompensating, I'm pretty sure that King Ahasuerus would drive a duallie. When we read through the list of the seven eunuchs who served the king, I can't help but wonder why he employs so many. If the king's orders are always obeyed, and if he is a man to be feared or respected, then why would he appoint these eunuchs to attend him?

Maybe it is because his orders might not always be followed and that he is afraid that his authority would be questioned. Perhaps this king needed to be reminded of his own sense of power. What better way to guarantee both of those things than to surround oneself with eunuchs? We do know that eunuchs (castrated males) were considered to be safe, or suitable, to be in the service of kings considering the number of women in a king's harem. Still, so many eunuchs in addition to other advisors as this king had seems to be another mark of his self-importance.

So here we are on the seventh day. We find the king "merry with wine." In other words, Ahasuerus is drunk. In his drunken state, he instructs his attending eunuchs to fetch Queen Vashti, adorned in her royal garb and crowning jewels. He wishes to show off his most beautiful possession, his wife. Just as the previous passages describe the beauty of the violet fabrics and silver curtain hangers, Vashti was called to appear as another lovely ornament in the king's court.

Here we are faced with another challenge in interpretation. We have a picture of a drunken man and his desire to exploit his wife. We could easily turn this passage into an advertisement for the snares and traps of mass alcohol consumption and drunkenness, or the dangers of marrying a power-hungry doofus. But that is not what the author intends. We cannot commit the mistake of inserting meaning where there is none. This is not to negate the sin of drunkenness, nor the tragedy of spousal exploitation.

However, this is an opportunity to seek out what the author is trying to convey. Adding the detail that Ahasuerus was "merry with wine," and that he summoned Vashti as a result, imparts the message that he might not have made the decision to summon her had he been sober.

We commit error when we seek to imitate actions, or actions of people, found in the text when divorced from their meaning. So, while this text may have been used as a warning for drunkenness or spousal mistreatment, that is not its primary aim. The aim of this passage is to communicate the story of what happened.

We have many tools available to help us understand what is happening within the text. My "go-to" resource is the use of a Bible commentary.

DO YOU HAVE ACCESS TO RESOURCES THAT CAN HELP AID YOU IN YOUR SEARCH FOR CONTEXT AND MEANING, LIKE A COMMENTARY?

A commentary is a resource book that has comments on and explanations of biblical texts. My favorite commentary is *The Moody Bible Commentary* edited by Michael Rydelnik and Michael Vanlaningham. These resource books are great and should be included in your own Bible study tool kit. And as an aside, when consulting a commentary, it's important to choose one written by someone who acknowledges Scripture as the inerrant Word of God. You'll want to do a little background into the publisher and editor of a commentary to ensure it's a trustworthy resource.

As was the custom, Vashti was hosting a separate banquet for the women of the court. The text doesn't say why Vashti refuses the summons, but she does. All we really know about Vashti is that "she was lovely to look at." She disobeys the king and this response spins him into a rage.

We don't know why she refused. All we know is that she did. While sexism is not the theme of the book of Esther, and we should refrain from viewing the text through the lens of that interpretation, we still can glean wisdom and understanding from topics presented in the text. Sexism is an issue that we are still dealing with today. Women all over the world are objectified and exploited. I think that we can put this truth in our back pocket. **You don't have to provide a reason or give an explanation in order to avoid being exploited.**

WHY DO YOU THINK THAT AHASUERUS SUMMONED VASHTI TO THE FEAST?

In researching this question, I found several possible causes. One commentary suggested that she would be asked to dance for the king and his guests. Another suggested that Vashti would have to arrive in her royal garb, something that would have taken her a substantial time to prepare.

Since the Scripture is sparse with the details about Vashti's refusal, we can't declare with certainty what was behind it. But one thing is sure. She was called on to be looked at, ogled even, for the pleasure of the king's guests, tantamount to a contemporary woman being asked to appear skimpily clad at a party attended by drunken men. Vashti refused.

Vashti's refusal is a triple threat. She is a woman refusing the authority of a man, a wife refusing the orders of her husband, and further, she is a subject rebelling against her sovereign. This defiance is the trifecta of disobedience and insubordination.

When his command was refused, the king seethed with rage. The passage says that "his anger burned within him."

While I don't particularly love Ahasuerus's character, I can relate to him. He's obsessive about his image and he's an angry guy. I can be obsessive about how people perceive me, and my default setting is "angry."

Many times, we like to identify ourselves with biblical heroes, or with the people described in God's stories as "righteous." However, we are usually quite the opposite. When faced with challenges, we are not David, slaying our own Goliaths, but we are unfaithful Israel, wandering about and perpetually lost.

HAVE YOU EVER IDENTIFIED WITH A "BIBLICAL HERO OR HEROINE"? WHICH ONE?

If we are honest with ourselves, we would have to admit that we are most like the messy, mischievous, or even malicious mistake makers recorded throughout the history of the Bible. Their stories are our stories.

Let's make sure to understand the climate here; the social, political, and relational climate of this story. Here is the king, hosting a lavish and decadent party, attempting to win the approval of his war council, who views his wife as a possession. His possession, meaning Vashti, disobeys him in public. This damages his image and hurts his pride. It seems like this guy is trying to control everything but himself. I think of this guy as a textbook narcissist.

A narcissist, or a person suffering from Narcissistic Personality Disorder, is defined by the Mayo Clinic as a person who has "a mental condition in which people have an inflated sense of their own importance, a deep need for excessive attention and admiration, troubled relationships, and a lack of empathy for others. But behind the mask of extreme confidence lies a fragile self-esteem that's vulnerable to the slightest criticism."[4]

IN WHAT WAYS MIGHT AHASUERUS SEEM SOMEWHAT NARCISSISTIC?

Let's see what happens when Ahasuerus, and his narcissistic plan, is foiled. Read verses 13–15.

Ahasuerus is about to exact his revenge through the law and shift the blame. He is quick to act in his hurt and is about to be irrational. He seeks input from experts in Persian law for backup. "Since it was customary for the king to consult experts in matters of law and justice, he spoke with the wise men who understood the times and were closest to the king" (v. 13–14 NIV). Then, in addition, by enacting the law, he shifts the responsibility to manage his own anger to the law of the land.

Revenge is tough. It keeps our hearts trapped in the darkness, away from the light of forgiveness. English philosopher and statesman Francis Bacon, in his essay "On Revenge," said this: "A man that studieth revenge keeps his wounds green, which otherwise, would heal and do well."[5] Ahasuerus is bent on retribution.

Probably each of us can remember a time when someone caused us great pain. It's especially hurtful when it's a person we had been close to, and even worse when they try to get others in our circle of friends on their side. We want nothing more than to defend ourselves and get even. And maybe you've done that.

On reflection, revenge is a toxic cancer. It forces us to focus only on ourselves and tempts us to take justice into our own hands. Revenge is an altar we build to ourselves and on it, we slice away at our own flesh, bleeding out, under the misconception that we are healing.

ARE YOU HARBORING THOUGHTS OF REVENGE? TAKE A SECOND TO JOT DOWN YOUR THOUGHTS ON HOW TO PUT THEM AWAY.

FIND 1 THESSALONIANS 5:15, 2 CORINTHIANS 13:11 (in the original language, "brothers" is not exclusively male, but also implies "sisters"), AND HEBREWS 10:30. COPY THEM HERE.

The Bible is pretty clear about how we are to handle feelings of revenge. We are to strive for peace and reconciliation.

We finish up today with King Ahasuerus seeking to find the punishment for Vashti's refusal, and what comes next will be sharp. We've watched what happens when pride and anger shove their way in, and we can see we why we should fight against such urges. As we close, take a moment to scribble down a prayer of repentance, asking God to help us in our need of Him.

As a side note, narcissism and marriage make for trying times. This is not a study about marriage, nor will we spend an inordinate amount of time on the topic. But in my years as a women's minister and shepherd, I have found that women who are suffering from the words and actions of a narcissistic spouse need to be assured of a few things.

Their behavior is not your fault, you do not deserve what you are enduring, nor is it God's will for husbands to mistreat or abuse their wives.

God's vision for marriage is one of mutual submission to Jesus as Lord and manifests in a respectful, tender, loving lifestyle of sacrificial living.

If you are finding yourself frustrated or suffering long, be encouraged. You are not without resources or help. Reach out to women in leadership at your church, find a counselor, or search for ministries in your local area that may be able to help. You can cling to the truth that the Lord loves you deeply and is wholly with you right now.

Take a moment to pray over today's reading and jot down your thoughts.

WEEK 1 | DAY 4

READ ESTHER CHAPTER 1.

SCRIPTURE FOCUS: Esther 1:16–20

Power, when doused with pride and arrogance, is like gasoline poured on wildfire. In November of 2018, Butte County in California endured a wildfire that was sparked by a faulty ignition line. It burned through 153,336 acres and 18,804 structures, resulting in eighty-five deaths. It is hard to contemplate this level of damage and death.

Pride, on its own, is an incendiary sin. It's one that is nursed by its keeper, and the flames are fanned by narcissism and vanity. Give unlimited power to pride, and the scorching flames rise higher and higher, consuming everything in its path.

We find the king's good spirits interrupted by rejection and rage. In his efforts to find wise counsel, he solicits the help and advice of Memucan. What he gets in return is nothing short of absurd.

I occasionally suffer with mild anxiety and struggle with fear. I am terribly afraid of really ridiculous things. Bridges send me into an almost inconsolable state. I have seriously researched minivan seats that also double as life flotation devices. I mean, with four children and only two arms, isn't this a slightly legitimate fear? Maybe? No? Okay . . .

While I may be slightly ridiculous in my fear of long-lasting overpasses and bridges, Memucan has a full-blown freak-out over a woman in opposition to a man's authority.

WHAT IS MEMUCAN'S MESSAGE VV. 16–18? WHAT IS HE AFRAID WILL HAPPEN?

That is a pretty specific fear: women everywhere will hear of Vashti's refusal and revolt, from the noblewoman (v. 18) to the commoner (v. 20).

READ V. 19. WHY DO YOU THINK MEMUCAN'S RESPONSE IS SO HARSH?

Queen Vashti was being summoned to be exploited for her beauty and for the pleasure of others. In response to her refusal, men who were seeking to sexualize or objectify her are now deeply offended. Memucan in particular is so offended that Vashti would not subject herself to being his eye candy that he predicted wives throughout the empire would react in similar ways to husbands' demands. It would almost be a comical scene were it not so troubling.

His goal is simple. He intends to prey on the king's own vanity and fear in order to strip Vashti of her royal title and manipulate the king into acting. Memucan wants to make an example of Vashti.

SO WHAT IS MEMUCAN'S SOLUTION (V. 19)?

"Isn't it ironic?" I'm singing this song in my head as I write the next sentence. It's ironic that the punishment for not appearing before the king is to never appear before the king again.

This guy is smart. "You *can't* quit—you're fired!" Yeah, that's a weird flex, bro. This verdict also elevates him in the sight of the king. By exaggerating the magnitude of this offense, Memucan and the other nobility solidify their own significance to the king by guaranteeing his reliance on them.

HAVE YOU EVER OVERREACTED TO A PERCEIVED OFFENSE?

IF SO, DID YOU CONFESS AND SEEK RECONCILIATION, OR DID YOU PRETEND THAT IT NEVER HAPPENED?

IN ADDITION, WHAT DID THIS EXPERIENCE TEACH YOU ABOUT SEEKING WISE COUNSEL?

These questions may feel a bit probing, or even unnecessary, but in order to grow spiritually, we have to free ourselves from the notion that we are perfect people, not prone to error and misjudgment. In order to grow, we need to open ourselves to the conviction, truth, and healing that comes through what God's Word reveals about us.

There will be times where schemes are recklessly created, and they cause damage. Maybe we are the ones doing the scheming, or maybe we are those whom the scheme will hurt most. **Schemes and their outcomes, no matter how disastrous, don't change God's love for us.**

Schemes, failed plans, pain, and suffering are all parts of the human experience outside of heaven. We can count on them to happen, the same as we can count on the sun to rise. And just as we can count on the sun to rise, we can also rely on the Lord to be with us through hardship. God is not apathetic or distant. He is all-knowing. He sees everything and nothing is wasted. None of the pain, none of the tears, and none of the hurt is too far from redemption.

WEEK 1 | DAY 5

READ ESTHER CHAPTER 1.

SCRIPTURE FOCUS: Esther 1:19–22

I often ponder how Vashti handled her harsh dismissal. In addition to her title being stripped away, she is to be *replaced* with someone "better." Is her replacement to be more beautiful, more subservient? She could not have had any idea that her dethroning would play a role in the deliverance of an entire people, nor could she have predicted the events to come. Vashti is about to be dethroned, clearing the way for the story to unfold.

But what about our "dethroning"? Does it feel unfair or like a punishment? Can we trust God with our failures and fallouts or, as in Vashti's case, the unfair treatment of others? Vashti may not have known the Lord, but we do. We can trust that He is in control and that what He has for us is better than anything we could conjure up in our feeble and finite minds.

Is it true that we are loved by God *only* when things are in our favor?

Or is the truth that failures and fallouts are just part of life on this side of eternity? We have to stop accepting the lie from hell that says, "You are only loved when things go your way." We will certainly fail and there will most definitely be pain during our time on earth. God's love is not limited to when we feel seen and cared for, but His love is also ever-present in the midst of dashed dreams, failed plans, and flayed hopes. His love is not always shown in the ways we succeed, the places where we shine, or in the relationships we exalt in. However, it is always shown in His promises, namely in the promise and sacrifice of Jesus.

DO YOU TRUST GOD WHEN THINGS GO WRONG?

WHAT ARE THE THINGS THAT CAUSE YOU TO DOUBT HIS PRESENCE?

Here's the truth. Even when we can't see God, discern His purpose, or feel His presence, we can trust that He is with us and that He is in control. During what Spanish priest John of the Cross (1542–1591) famously referred to as the "dark night of the soul," we can begin to trust that God cares and that nothing will be wasted.

You may not be able to see what God is doing, or where He is moving in your life, but trust that He is indeed active. You are deeply and fiercely loved by the God of the universe. He has pursued you and has called you His from the beginning of time.

So, it was declared throughout the kingdom that Vashti was never to come before the king again and "the king did as Memucan proposed" (v. 21).

The purpose of this strange and egotistical edict was to make an example out of Vashti and to frighten women into honoring their husbands. Basically, Memucan and Ahasuerus wanted all husbands to rule their household with an iron fist and a demand for honor.

The marriage between Vashti and Ahasuerus—more than likely contracted for political gain rather than a love match—is far from our contemporary understanding of marriage. Still, it's worth taking some of the events from this account to delve into what we can learn from the passage. The concept of *demanding* honor, respect, and submission is in complete opposition to what the apostle Paul writes in Ephesians regarding marriage.

FIND EPHESIANS 5:22-33.

In this text, both husbands and wives are given instructions on how to approach the task of biblical marriage. We are going to camp out here for just a moment because, in my many years of ministry, this passage has caused much confusion and heartache.

"Wives, submit to your own husbands, as to the Lord." (Ephesians 5:22)

In some circles, this is typically about as much as women will hear on the subject of submission. You submit and that is it. There is usually little to no discussion of the responsibility of husbands, nor is there always a resounding call for men to answer the responsibility of biblical marriage.

Let's unpack this so that we can have a better understanding, and so that we can see the vast contrast between Ahasuerus's idea of what a marriage relationship means and the type of marriage Christians are actually called to.

First of all, there are three couplets in this passage from Ephesians. A wife's submission is linked with a husband's sacrifice. A metaphor is used to depict the nature of a whole body—the husband as a head and the wife as the body. Then, another couplet is used to link a husband's love to a wife's respect.[6]

Second, if you were to read the passage in its original language, Greek, you would find that verse 22 states, "Wives to your own husbands . . ." Wives what? There is no verb in the sentence. What are wives supposed to do? To find the answer, you would have to read Ephesians 5:21, which says, "submitting to one another out of reverence to Christ."

Biblical marriage is rooted and foundationally built on a mutual submission to Christ. Husbands submit to Christ by loving their wives and treating them like their own bodies, through nurturing care and sacrifice. Wives submit to Christ by their submission to their husbands—husbands who sacrifice for them—and by giving them respect.

The church makes an error when the biblical teaching on Christian marriage is misunderstood or misapplied as a doctrine of male dominance and abuse.

This "hammer and nail" relationship okayed here by King Ahasuerus could not be further from God's design of love and marriage. His heart is for men and women to love Him, and out of the abundance of that love, to love each other. So much so that this particular love, in marriage, is cited as a picture of the gospel of Christ and the church for our world today.

The last part of today's passage reads, "This advice pleased the king and the princes, and the king did as Memucan proposed. He sent letters to all the royal provinces, to every province in its own script and to every people in its own language, that every man be master in his own household and speak according to the language of his people" (vv. 21–22).

The king called up the Persian Pony Express to carry the news of his humiliation to the four corners, even going to the lengths of translating his decree into all the languages of the people. We can learn a few things from this snippet of Scripture. First, we see that Persian laws were irrevocable. Second, we can gather that this postal service of fast horses and swift riders played a very important part in carrying out the king's edicts.

As we wrap up this chapter in Esther, we are being invited to see things differently. We are being encouraged to see the long game, the big picture, even when we have no idea what is to come or how things will turn out. The Lord is sweetly calling us to rest in Him, to trust that He has everything in hand.

Can you trust God with what He has in front of you today? Take a moment to jot down a few thoughts about what you can surrender to His control and how you can learn to trust Him.

SUMMONED
to Seek

WEEK 2 | DAY 1

READ ESTHER CHAPTER 2.

SCRIPTURE FOCUS: Esther 2:1–4

Have you ever stepped away from a dramatic situation and, on reflection, regretted your part in the scuffle? That's what is happening now for our not-so-favorite king.

A few years back, I got into a pretty heated argument with a friend. She crossed boundaries, and I found myself treading across a few lines myself. It was more than heated. Accusations were thrown at me like knives, and like any smart person in a knife fight, I threw up my arms (and maybe a few of my own sucker punches) in defense. Long story short, the friendship ended sharply. A few years later, I remembered her and how my behavior could have been better. I had made a mistake, and I missed my friend.

HAVE YOU EVER MADE A RELATIONSHIP MISTAKE THAT YOU "REMEMBERED"?

HOW DID YOU FEEL ABOUT THE WAY THINGS PANNED OUT?

The Scripture says that Ahasuerus "remembered Vashti and what she had done and what had been decreed against her" (Esther 2:1).

We pick up from last week and, by Esther 2, the king has cooled off. According to historical sources, around this time Ahasuerus headed off to war with Greece and suffered a humiliating defeat. At the start of Esther 2, four years had gone by since Vashti was dethroned, and we find the king back home in Persia, defeated in battle, low in spirit, and missing his wife.

As a side note, this word "remembered" was typically used in the Old Testament to describe Israel reflecting on God's goodness and faithfulness.

It is ironic that the author would choose that word here.

Let's look at the timeline.

DURING WHAT YEAR OF KING AHASUERUS'S REIGN DID THIS STORY BEGIN (SEE ESTHER 1:3)?

Many times, we make the mistake of reading the Bible like we would watch a movie—in the span of an hour and a half, we are able to piece together the plot, be entertained, note that each conflict is resolved, and rejoice that everyone lives happily ever after. When reading the Bible, we don't always consider the vast amount of real time that passes between passages. When we do this, we rush the text and miss the things God is trying to reveal to us through story. This story began in the third year of Ahasuerus's reign. We are now approaching the end of his sixth year. Almost four years have passed since Vashti's banishment, and much has happened, albeit that most of what happened in those years is not recorded in the Scriptures.

So here sits King Ahasuerus, longing for his dethroned and dismissed wife. He understands the irrevocable nature of Persian laws, and despite any of his private or personal feelings, she is gone for good. In an effort to distract him from his current woes, and really the consequences of his own hasty and harsh decree, his "young men" suggest that he make good on his plan to replace Vashti.

What better way to get over your current heartache than to ignite the lust within and meet someone new, right? This was the thought process of the king's men. And the Scripture says that this suggestion "pleased the king, and he did so."

As we venture deeper into this particular passage, buckle your seat belt and hold on tight. We are headed into dark and sinister territory. In many ways, we are about to get a glimpse of evil—an evil that is alive and well today.

Before we trudge forward, let's look at the story of Esther that many of us may have heard as children. It may have sounded something like this:

"Once upon a time, there was a beautiful young girl. She had long flowing hair and was very appealing. She fell in love with a handsome king and won a kingdom-wide beauty pageant to win his heart. They were married and she saved God's people from a bad man in court." The message could be "Be brave like Esther" or "Be kind and lovable like Esther."

Let me be clear: *this is not that story*. There are no tiaras and pretty dresses here in this passage, only kidnapping, sex trafficking, and mass mutilation.

HOW HAS THE STORY OF ESTHER BEEN PRESENTED TO YOU, PERHAPS AS A CHILD IN SUNDAY SCHOOL OR ELSEWHERE?

The sanitized-for-children version of brave Queen Esther is one of a tragic case of scriptural misuse. While well-meaning children's ministers and parents seek to clean up this tale of woe, the truth remains that there is no cutesy image that could portray the horrors held within these events.

At this point in the text, the king's men have suggested the systematic "gathering" of attractive women, over the expanse of an entire kingdom, for the purpose of what was basically sexual slavery.

What King Ahasuerus's men were suggesting would include the kidnapping, and subsequent sexual exploitation, of countless women across 127 provinces (Esther 1:1).

The Persian Empire was only slightly smaller than the size of the entire United States. Imagine every state, city, metroplex, and backwoods country town seizing women by the authority of appointed "officers" and turning them over to government harems.

Another gruesome detail in this epilogue is that, in order to care for this immense intake of sex slaves, young men were also rounded up and castrated en masse.

Eunuchs were needed to keep charge of the new "labor force." In his records, the historian Herodotus estimates that as many as five hundred young men were gathered each year, castrated, and entered into service at the Persian court.[1]

DO THE DETAILS OF THIS STORY CHANGE THE PERCEPTION YOU MAY HAVE HAD BEFORE ABOUT THE STORY OF ESTHER?

We have to develop the skill of digging deeper into the text in order to develop better biblical interpretation. This vital and essential skill will be the difference between life and death. When we only adhere to the minimal messages held within the children's versions of these narratives, we will miss the mark. We have to excavate the text, through the lenses of cultural understanding and context, to really grasp the truth of God's Word.

The book of Esther also teaches us that the Bible doesn't shy away from hard things. This book, which begins with the systematic sexual trauma of what could be thousands of men and women, invites us to see the hand of God moving through the most deplorable and depraved of conditions.

WHAT ARE SOME QUESTIONS THAT COME TO YOUR MIND WHEN READING ABOUT THESE EVENTS?

Some of you may be asking yourselves how God could watch all this suffering and not intervene. You might be asking why people treat each other so abhorrently. Still, some of you might be processing the shock of the mass amount of trauma being inflicted on these men and women.

Here is the truth. God is bigger. He is bigger than sin. He is bigger than evil. He can work in and through some of the most unfathomable places and people.

The book of Esther is an invitation to see things differently, to see things through a worldview that elevates God's faithfulness even when the circumstances surrounding us blur our vision and break our hearts.

IS THERE A SITUATION IN YOUR LIFE WHERE YOU STRUGGLE TO SEE GOD'S FAITHFULNESS BECAUSE OF HARD OR HEAVY CIRCUMSTANCES?

When we see things in this life that shake us to our very core, we can rest in the truth that none of our pain, our sacrifices, or our circumstances get the last say. We are not abandoned children who are wandering waywardly alone. Instead, we are most loved in that God sees all and loves us in spite of hurt or hardship.

WEEK 2 | DAY 2

READ ESTHER CHAPTER 2.

SCRIPTURE FOCUS: Esther 2:5–14

Before we begin to unpack this passage, we have to talk about the land. Jerusalem was a symbol of God's faithfulness and a place where His presence dwelled with the people. Everything about Jewish culture, tradition, and identity was tied to the promised land, specifically the temple. When Nebuchadnezzar of Babylon conquered the holy city, the temple was razed to the ground and God's people were exiled.[2] This exile was a punishment, the consequence of their unfaithfulness and idolatry. The term for this period is *diaspora*.

Diaspora is the dispersion of the Jews from Israel, from the promised land, which has occurred many times in history. The word "diaspora" comes from a Greek word meaning "to be scattered about." It is through these lenses, the lenses of diaspora, that we must approach the story of Esther.

This is why we find Mordecai, and many other Jewish people, living in Persia.

WHAT IS MORDECAI'S GENEALOGY (ESTHER 2:5)?

Mordecai is introduced with a list of his genealogy. **Here's a tip. Whenever you see someone being introduced with a lengthy list of ancestors, pay attention. It denotes importance.** He is a Benjaminite, and his ancestry can be traced all the way back to 1100 BC, to Kish—King Saul's father.

In the Hebrew, verses 5–6 read like this:

"Now there was a Jew in Susa the citadel whose name was Mordecai, the son of Jair, son of Shimei, son of Kish, a Benjaminite, who had been [*exiled*] away from Jerusalem among the captives [was *exiled*] with Jeconiah king of Judah, whom Nebuchadnezzar king of Babylon had [*exiled*]."

Notice any pattern here?

WHAT RELATIONSHIP DOES ESTHER (HADASSAH) HAVE TO MORDECAI?

It is interesting to note that both of these names, Mordecai and Esther, have Persian roots. The name Mordecai, or the Persian Marduk, means "man of Marduk." Marduk was the chief god in the Babylonian pantheon of gods. In the same way, the name Esther could have been a nod to Ishtar, the Persian goddess of love and war; it could also derive from "star" in Persian.

Why is this important? Well, it shows their detachment from their Jewish roots. It also indicates that they were born in exile, which means their connection with the Holy Land is separated by time *and* distance. Because the Jewish way of life was connected to the temple, dietary restrictions, and living a lifestyle distinct from the Gentiles, this also means that most likely Mordecai and Esther have abandoned their dedication to Jewish Law written in the Torah.[3]

The Scripture says Esther was an orphan and Mordecai was the nephew of her father, so they are cousins. He brought her up as his own daughter (v. 7), and when the decree went out from the king and Esther was taken, the original language could be more aptly interpreted as *seized*.

Where is God? Esther's parents are dead and now she is being seized into the hands of a temperamental drunkard king for his harem, to be called to his presence for sex whenever he wished. How is this good news? Is she being punished? Or is there a different question that we are asking: ***When bad things happen, if God is all-knowing and all-powerful, why doesn't He intervene?***

Let's wrestle with this one for a minute. In countless places across Scripture, this question is posed, the question of "God, aren't You coming?" We have to grapple with the truth that God does not always rescue, and sometimes He doesn't move when and where and how we want Him to.

When we ask God to "fix it all," the hunger, the hate, and all the rest, we place our humanity above our sovereign and all-powerful God, insisting that He serve our interests and well-being above all else. Here is another question we can ask instead.

How can an all-knowing, all-seeing God, who knows the darkest and dirtiest things about me, continue to invite me to seek Him out of love through the death and resurrection of Jesus?

I want you to hear me say this: God has not abandoned us in our need, nor should His silence be taken as indifference. I am certain His heart was breaking at the sight of these women being forcibly taken from their homes and that heaven wept at the mass mutilation of God's people.

Some traditions of religious and philosophical thought say, "Good things happen to good people" and "Bad things happen to bad people." But does that line up with what we know to be true?

WHAT DO YOU THINK? DO YOU BELIEVE IN SOME FORM OF "YOU GET WHAT YOU GIVE" TYPE OF BELIEF?

I don't know about you, but I certainly don't want to get what I deserve all of the time. Being human means to fail, to make mistakes, to hurt, and be hurt. The truth is that none of us who believe in the sacrificial death and miraculous resurrection of Jesus will get what we deserve in the end. Jesus has already taken the punishment for it all.

While religions may tout blanket statements about simplistic issues of "good" and "evil," we Christians can firmly assert that sin has touched everything and everyone.

FIND ROMANS 3 AND READ VERSES 23–27. WHAT DO YOU LEARN FROM THIS PASSAGE?

The truth of it is this: none of us really want what we deserve. Romans 3 says "None is righteous," not even one person, and "All have turned aside" (vv. 10, 12). None of us have gotten it right and none of us deserve the grace that God has given us in and through the cross of Christ. All of us are broken sinners without Him. Romans 6:23 says "The wages of sin is death." The wages of our sins have been eternally paid by Jesus. The debt is paid, and the slate is clean.

We can still ask God why He doesn't crash in at every turn, when we want Him to save us or stop something hard. But if we are too attached to an outcome—rather than His will or greater plan—we will always be disappointed. Let's say this again: if we are more attached to a desired outcome of our difficulties than living in His will or in accordance with His plan, we will certainly be disappointed.

The bottom line is that even if God never intervened on our behalf for anything else, two thousand years ago on the hill of Calvary, He gave us His Son. And through Jesus, we have an unshakable hope—a hope that can carry us through the pain and suffering of life on this side of heaven.

I wonder what Esther was thinking as she entered into the harem gates. Being handed over to Hegai, the head eunuch in charge of the women, sounds unfamiliar, vulnerable, and scary. Even so, Scripture says she "pleased him and won his favor" (Esther 2:9). Even now, we are seeing the unseen God moving in and through this terrible situation, providing provision for Esther.

Do you think He moves for us too?

HAVE YOU BEEN IN A SITUATION WHERE YOU COULD LOOK BACK AND SEE HIS SOVEREIGN HAND?

As I mentioned earlier, several years ago my husband deployed to the Middle East, leaving me all alone with three young children. I was struggling with postpartum depression, and I wasn't sure who I was anymore. We had moved more times than I could count, I couldn't hold down a career because of all the moving, and I had lost purpose. That season was one of the darkest of our marriage. I was hurt and resentful. Many times, I wondered if I could survive my life as a military spouse. I remember begging the Lord to help me make it to 8:00 p.m. (bedtime) and to bring some small measure of peace.

Looking back, I can clearly see His hand with me through every obstacle— guiding and shepherding me. I can see how that season strengthened my marriage and equipped me for ministry. God had brought me to the end of myself so that I could see my great need for Him. I couldn't do it on my own. I was not enough (I'm still not). The good news is that I don't *have* to be and neither do you. Why? Because Jesus is enough. Through His perfect life, sacrificial death, and powerful resurrection we have access to God. We can come with these burdens and hardships because there is no longer an endless separation between us. Because of Jesus, nothing is wasted.

When we look at the story of Esther, we are forced to look at the depths of the ugliness that lies within humanity. Sometimes, the harsh and horrible things that happen are happening to us. Other times, we can be the cause of them. Many times, we are uncertain or unsure about what to do when we find ourselves in the midst of madness.

WHAT DID ESTHER CHOOSE TO KEEP HIDDEN? (ESTHER 2:10)

Why would Esther hide her heritage? Was she afraid, or was there a good reason to lie about her identity? Find Ezra 4:1–6. Apparently, there were accusations circulating about the Jewish community and reason to fear that exposure could be dangerous.

At this point in the story, Esther is hiding. She is hiding her identity and in, what I imagine to be, survival mode.

Haven't we all been in this survival mode before, where we are striving to simply stay afloat among the winds and waves of life? I constantly feel like the circumstances surrounding the active duty military life throws me violently into survival mode.

WHO OR WHAT DO WE TURN TO IN THESE SEASONS?

While Esther didn't have control over her circumstances, she did have support. Today's Scripture focus says that Mordecai walked in front of the court of the harem every day, in order to see how she was doing and what was happening (2:11).

While this one line of text at the surface level doesn't seem to have much to offer, when I read this Scripture, I see a dedication most women crave today.

Do we have someone who genuinely cares about our well-being? Do we have someone in our lives who is so deeply concerned that they alter their plans, make allowances, and include us in their daily routine?

Do you have such a person? If you do, take a moment to jot down a prayer of thanksgiving to God. If not, take a moment to ask your Father for a person like this. Ask God to send someone into your life who can meet this need. Maybe even ask God who might need you to show up for them in this way.

As we finish up today's reading, I want to encourage you to reach out.

So many times, I hear women say that the sting of loneliness is so painful. The pain is so immense that they find it difficult to feel loved by God. We can do something about this. We can solve this problem, one connection at a time. Be intentional. Seek out opportunities to connect with someone else. Be the voice of comfort, the show of support, or the hand of peace for others. We were made for love, to serve one another.

HOW CAN YOU ENCOURAGE SOMEONE TODAY?

If we can glean anything from Mordecai today, it would be to notice his heart and dedication to Esther. We, through the power of the Holy Spirit, can have and give this dedication. Ask yourself what your greatest need is today and then ask the same question of someone close to you. Pray for God to grant you the opportunity to serve someone else and for Him to send someone to minister to you too.

WEEK 2 | DAY 3

READ ESTHER CHAPTER 2.

SCRIPTURE FOCUS: Esther 2:5–14

Who is this Hegai guy? We unpacked a ton of the text yesterday, but I want to take a second to talk about this dude. Hegai is the king's eunuch, in charge of the women. He manages the women in the king's house and is in charge of their upkeep. The thing that I find most interesting about our boy Hegai is that he was a Gentile (the word Jews used for someone who was not a Jew) who knew nothing of the King of heaven. Nevertheless, he was used in God's plan.

Isn't it amazing that God is so powerful, so sovereign, and so magnanimous that He can work His plan in and through the thoughts and deeds of an Old Testament harem keeper?

Have you ever thought that you are too messed up, too sinful, or too far away for God to use you? Let Hegai be a resounding testimony to thwart that lie from hell. God can crash in when and wherever He wants. But imagine what life could be like if we actively invited Him in and acknowledged the lordship of Jesus in our lives.

IS THERE SOMETHING YOU NEED TO STOP AND CONFESS HERE? HAVE YOU MOVED AWAY FROM GOD BECAUSE YOU BELIEVED YOU WERE "TOO FAR GONE"?

Esther had won favor in the eyes of Hegai and he advanced Esther to the best place in the harem. He gives her the required beauty treatments and her portion of food. (This food, by the way, would most likely not be kosher, or prepared in accordance with the Jewish regulations.) She is being prepared to be handed over for a night with the king.

The word here for "cosmetics" in Hebrew is *tamruq*. It originates from the Hebrew word used to describe scouring, scraping, rubbing.[4] These women were hoarded together and subjected to a "purifying" treatment that would require them to soak in herbal baths and apply all types of tonics and lotions for an entire year. This was all done with one goal in mind: to please the king—a theme we see arise time and time again in the book of Esther.

We are told in the text that Esther continued to hide her identity as a Jewish woman. The food we mentioned earlier would violate the Law. The preparation for a one-night stand? It definitely went against her beliefs. Make no mistake, Esther was not in the palace harem by choice, nor did she feel like she had much room to reveal who she was. She was most certainly a victim.

We, on the other hand, do have a voice and a choice. But so many times, we too hide who we are. We sacrifice our principles and compromise our beliefs, all for the sake of fitting in or avoiding the prospect of offending someone. We aren't in any imminent danger for sharing our faith. We would just rather not.

HAVE YOU EVER FELT THE NEED TO COMPROMISE OR HIDE YOUR BELIEFS? WHY?

A popular saying that circulates in some Christian circles goes something like this—"Preach the gospel every day and, if need be, use words." This is one of the most misguided and frustrating sayings there is. The gospel requires words. In order to *tell* someone the truth about who Jesus is, we have to use our words.

The second verse to this "song" is that in order to "preach the gospel every day," we need to know the gospel.

HOW COMFORTABLE ARE YOU WITH SHARING THE REDEMPTIVE STORY OF THE GOSPEL?

Imagine this scene. Esther 2:12–14 paints a dreary picture. Women were being systematically subjected to sex slavery. These women were forcibly taken from their homes or sold, herded like cattle into herbal baths, used for sex, and then they could be set aside to live a lonely life in isolation as a concubine. Can you imagine the hurt, shame, and suffering?

Sadly, this scenario isn't limited to biblical times. The sex industry is still alive and well today. People in countries all over the world are profiting from and propagating sex slavery. One could even call trauma a mission field.

A few years ago, I had lunch with a friend who served as a missionary in Calcutta, India. She served in the red-light district and helped women escape the sex industry by teaching them to learn a trade. She shared such incredible and inspiring stories of hope, of redemption, through teaching the gospel.

HAVE YOU EVER CONSIDERED THAT GOD IS CALLING YOU, IN ONE WAY OR ANOTHER, TO SHARE THE GOSPEL WITH WOMEN SUCH AS THESE?

The longer I search through the book of Esther, the more I find a recurring truth, a difficult truth that makes its way to the front of my mind. **Everything that happens in this life is either *willed* or *allowed* by God.** All things, both the good and bad, the hard and the easy, and the life-giving and the tragic are *used* by God.

Let me be clear. God **did not** orchestrate Esther's rape, nor the systematic abuse of all of the other women in this story, for His glory.[5]

There is another story in the Old Testament that teaches us how God deals with the darkness of this world. In the book of Genesis, Joseph, a most beloved child of Rachel and Jacob, was sold into slavery by his jealous brothers. He was carried away to Egypt and was accused of violating his master's wife, though he never touched her and, in fact, rebuffed her advances toward him. Then he was thrown into prison and left to rot for years. After a series of events, Joseph was freed from prison and raised to a high position of power. He was given the tools by God to save many, including his brothers.

FIND GENESIS 50:20 AND WRITE IT HERE.

If you have headings listed in your Bible translation, something like "God's Good Purpose" might be fixed just above this passage of Scripture. The message here is this: God can and will use anything to accomplish His purposes, even the broken things of this world like sexual sin and slavery.

Here is the truth we can rest in: **God might not always prevent pain, but the glorious truth is that He always redeems it when we give it to Him.** We can bring our hurts and pains to Him. We can ask Him to redeem them, to help us deal with the fallout of the things that have happened to us.

I once heard pastor and author Bruce Martin say something that has always stayed with me. It went something like this: "Our greatest point of pain is usually tied to our greatest purpose." What would it look like if we took our aches and pains to the cross and submitted them to the authority of heaven? Who could we reach with the gospel we might not have thought of? Where could we go, as an ambassador for the cause of Christ, that others without our struggle could not?

WHERE ARE SOME OF THE PLACES YOU COULD GO FOR CHRIST THAT OTHERS CAN'T?

WHO ARE SOME OF THE PEOPLE YOU THINK GOD MIGHT BE CALLING YOU TO REACH, THROUGH YOUR OWN UNIQUE POINTS OF PAIN?

Dearest, friend, regardless of whatever your challenges are in this life, of whatever scars—visible or invisible—you carry; despite whomever or whatever has caused you the deepest pain, you can rest in this: **God has always been with you and He is with you today.** If you find yourself in the pit of despair or depression because of hard things, know you are the most seen and the most beloved.

Take some time to contemplate your own dark places and try to see how God has "meant good" for you. Use this space to pray, draw, doodle, or mind map how you can see God's hand in your life through the past and the present.

WEEK 2 | DAY 4

READ ESTHER CHAPTER 2.

SCRIPTURE FOCUS: Esther 2:15–18

When we look at Esther 2, we have to step away from our Western and modern perspectives, specifically as it relates to sex. We have to excavate the text to see what lies beneath. We need to consider the culture and the worldview in which the original audience would have understood the text. Esther was not in this position by choice. She didn't volunteer and, in the cultural system of the time, she had very little option to refuse.

We have come to the place in the story where it is Esther's turn. Others have gone before her, and there will most likely still be a few behind her. As abhorrent as the idea sounds, every night he wanted, Ahasuerus was being served a new virgin to appease his ravenous appetite for lust. Esther had one job—to please the king. She listened to Hegai and took with her the things she needed to accomplish her mission.

There has been some polarizing discussion surrounding this event. In some circles, Esther is considered a biblical heroine. Her courage and bravery helped deliver God's people from what would have been certain death.

On the other hand, some scholars say that Esther's place in Scripture is overrated or unnecessary. They assert she was a Jewish girl who willingly gave her virginity to a Gentile king, making her little more than a harlot.

WHAT DO YOU THINK OF ESTHER, HAVING STUDIED THIS FAR?

Some commentators have tried to say that nothing happened between Esther and King Ahasuerus, that there was no sexual contact. Others say that Esther was sinful, using sex as a tool to win the throne, to manipulate the king.

I subscribe to a third option. While I would not use the word "harlot," I would say that Esther was, in fact, both a heroine and a woman who gave her virginity to a Gentile king. She was forced into a sinful situation and she was raised to a position of power. The two facts are tied together. In this line of thinking, there is tremendous hope.

We can be flawed, used, bruised, or broken *and still* play a vital role in God's plan. Perfection is not the requirement.

We can also say with certainty that the way she was treated was not her fault. Calling it "rape" might seem startling and evoke the act of violence we associate with this crime today. However, her virginity *was* taken, and she was forced into a lifestyle that left her open and vulnerable. Unfortunately, sexual abuse continues today—and tragically, in some Christian churches or organizations, women who have come forward with these charges have not been believed. I therefore find it absolutely necessary to clearly communicate that victims of sexual assault or unwanted advances most certainly did not "have it coming."

When we read this text about the events that came to pass for Esther, we should be cautious of molding her into something she wasn't, either a perfect saint or a degraded prostitute. This passage should invoke feelings of empathy, of compassion. We have to be mindful of our own tendencies to simplistically label things one way or another. God works in and through all different kinds of circumstances, so much so that He is on the move within one of the darkest stories recorded in Scripture.

After her night with the king, the Scripture says she "won grace and favor." Esther was named the queen and officially replaced Vashti.

If we were to take the time to compare them, we would find that these two women were both beautiful. It was said that Vashti was "lovely to look at" (Esther 1:11).

WHAT WAS SAID OF ESTHER IN VERSE 2:7?

The author of this book took the extra time to give us a sneak peek into the fact that Esther would win the crown. In Persia, it is only what is on the surface that counts, and the author wanted to make sure the original readers knew Esther had the edge.

In verse 17, the ESV tells us King Ahasuerus "loved Esther" more than all the others. But the NIV put it like this: "Now the king was attracted to Esther more than to any of the other women."

I can't say it enough. This story is not a romantic drama of deep and abiding love between Esther and Ahasuerus.

Another key takeaway in this passage is the fact that this text does not invite us to copy or mimic Esther's behavior in our own lives; rather it invites us to find encouragement when we wind up in situations or circumstances where right and wrong aren't always so clear.

A few months ago, I was visiting a church and spotted a bulletin board hanging outside the children's area. The board was covered with bright pink paper and had the silhouette of what looked to be a 1950s housewife. The black cutout form of a woman boasted an A-line dress, modest collar line, a neat hairdo, and white construction paper pearls. The pearls had Bible verses printed on them and there were letters above the cutout that read "Modest, like Esther."

I threw up in my mouth a little.

Biblical literacy has been in steady decline among the church for years, but my heart broke at the sight of this pathetic interpretation of the story behind Esther. What message are we honestly trying to impart to young girls with this framework of understanding? Do we say things like, "Be like Esther; use your body to impress and subdue powerful men"? Or, in a worse example, we could teach girls that the end justifies the means. "If there is a man you want to marry, impress him with your sexual prowess and win yourself a ring."

No. We can't do that here. The author doesn't tell us what Esther did or how. There is no action that was praised by this book's author in order to give us something to grasp on to for instruction. There is just simply the fact that Esther went into the king's palace a virgin and she came out a queen.

So Esther pleased the king and he "set the royal crown on her head." Vashti is but a memory, and the king throws, you guessed it, another party.

WHAT WAS THIS FEAST CALLED (ESTHER 2:18)?

Have you ever heard the saying "Happy wife, happy life"? Well, it seems that the same is true of good ol' Ahasuerus. When he is crabby, women lose titles and laws bend others to his will. When he is happy, a "tax-free weekend" is decreed and he is willing to give away large gifts to those in his service. This fussy and fickle king will continue to be a centerpiece of this story as the plot thickens and schemes are hatched. Buckle in, girls. The ride is about to get wild.

WEEK 2 | DAY 5

READ ESTHER CHAPTER 2.

SCRIPTURE FOCUS: Esther 2:19–23

We find an interesting phrase at the beginning of this passage. The text opens with "When the virgins were gathered together the second time . . ." So what's going on? Virgins are being "gathered together" again?

WHY DO YOU THINK MORE WOMEN ARE BEING "GATHERED TOGETHER" BY THE KING?

Esther is now the queen, but old habits die hard. We can't very well expect the king to be so easily swayed to monogamy, can we? After years of slaking an insatiable thirst for beautiful, virgin women, we find the king back in the saddle of systematic sex slavery.

Meanwhile, when Mordecai was sitting at the king's gate, he overhears a plot on the king's life; a plot that was hatched by two angry eunuchs in the king's service. It seems as though this was a "right time, right place" kind of scenario. How fortunate that Mordecai is just patiently sitting around when two thugs decide to "lay hands" on the king.

IS THIS A SERENDIPITOUS COINCIDENCE, OR IS THERE SOMETHING LARGER HAPPENING HERE?

The king's gate was a place of law, courts if you will. Mordecai's presence at the gate indicates that he had been elevated to an official position. Maybe Esther had put in a good word for him to be promoted, or maybe through his own merit he earned a place at court. Either way, it is in this moment that King Ahasuerus's fate is in the hands of this Jewish man of Susa and his cousin, Esther.

WHAT DID ESTHER DO TO SAVE KING AHASUERUS'S LIFE?

WHAT COMMAND HAD MORDECAI GIVEN TO ESTHER (V. 20)?

Esther respected Mordecai, as the Scripture denotes that she "obeyed" him. She continued to keep her identity hidden. This repetition bids us to lean a little further in and really examine what is happening in the text. We have to pay attention to repeated phrases and rhythms that change.

WHY DO YOU THINK ESTHER WAS COMMANDED TO KEEP HER IDENTITY HIDDEN?

Let's take a look at what it would have meant to keep her identity a secret. She would have had to behave in such a way that her ethnicity as a Jew would not have been easily spotted. She would have dressed like a Persian, eaten like a Persian, and, if she was in the habit of observing rituals such as times of prayer, she likely would have done so secretly. She would have to make many sacrifices and compromise greatly to blend in as just another Persian woman.

Do we do this? Might we carry ourselves in such a way that we would be indistinguishable as a Christian?

IN WHAT WAYS SHOULD WE BE RADICALLY DIFFERENT THAN THE WORLD AROUND US?

FIND JOHN 13:34-35 AND COPY IT HERE.

HOW WILL PEOPLE "KNOW" US AS DISCIPLES OF CHRIST?

As you discovered, Jesus teaches us that it will be by our love we are recognized as His. It will not be by our own righteousness, the number of times we have attended church, or the sin struggles we do not fight. No. It will be by our love for one another.

When we think of love, we sometimes can make the mistake of using the word "tolerance" in its place. Love is not merely tolerance.

"Love is _____ and _____; love does not _____ or _____; it is not _____ or _____. It does not _____ on its _____ _____; it is not _____ or _____; it does not _____ at _____, but _____ _____. Love bears all things, believes all things, hopes all things, endures all things."

Take a moment and think about how we can walk away from patterns of comparison and conforming in order to move toward rhythms of grace and actions of love.

We should not only be different and separate from this world, but we should be radically loving. But how do we deal with so many of today's polarizing issues with love? Well, for starters, we have to eliminate this paradigm of having to be against something in order to be for something else.

Another shift that must occur in our hearts is the desire to group people together, under labels of sorts. We cannot ultimately decide that we will hate these people or that group. Why not? Because love is not "arrogant or rude." It does not allow us to puff ourselves up and pat ourselves on the back for being "more righteous" or "holier" than others. The truth is that without Christ, we are all a mess and, if God counted our sins, the pile would rise to the heavens.

Last, we must recklessly abandon the habit of rejoicing in wrongdoing. We have a terrible habit of celebrating sinfulness in our culture. When a mighty person falls, we are usually some of the first to cheer. When a sharp disagreement rises between two opposing sides, we might be the first to throw on some popcorn and pull up a chair.

If love is the measurement that Jesus is telling us we will be recognized by, are we like Esther, hiding our identity and passing as just another Persian?

HOW CAN YOU BE MORE LOVING?

IS THERE A SIN STRUGGLE TO CONFESS?

CAN YOU THINK OF ONE WAY TO BEGIN TO WALK IN LOVE AND GRACE?

As we get ready to push into the next few chapters, we are going to be faced with hard topics. The Bible doesn't let us escape from subjects that may make us a bit squeamish. In the days ahead, we are going to see hatred and racism from the ruling authorities, and we'll deal with the suffering these two things leave in their wake.

Mordecai's discovery of the plot on the king's life at the end of chapter 2 is strategically settled between one conflict resolution and the real problem held within the text. This tiny piece of information in this passage will become a crucial point in the upcoming weeks.

Mordecai reveals this plot to Esther, and she relays it in his name. The king is saved and the event is recorded in the king's chronicles. As we'll see, Esther's influence with the king was strengthened by this incident.[6]

Usually, it was customary to reward a subject for something of this magnitude. Yet, we see no reward being given. Mordecai was most likely offended, or at the very least, he waited for an extended period of time for what he believed was due to him. We will see how this perceived slight will play out soon. But for now, let's just say our timing and desires don't always line up with the plans that God has in His own perfect timing.

WHAT IS ONE THING YOU HAVE TAKEN FROM TODAY'S READING?

SUMMONED

to Scrutinize

WEEK 3 | DAY 1

READ ESTHER CHAPTER 3.

SCRIPTURE FOCUS: Esther 3:1–4

We left off last week after Mordecai, with the help of Esther, saved the king from a violent assassination. He had overheard two disgruntled eunuchs planning to "lay hands" on the king, and because Mordecai was in the right place at the right time, he was able to intercede. The king is delivered from the hands of angry men and the event is recorded in the chronicles in the king's presence.

Today, our Scripture focus begins again with an indicator of time. The events in chapter 3 begin about five years after those in the first two chapters.

What are the first three words of Esther 3? Fill in the blanks.

_____ King Ahasuerus promoted Haman the Agagite, the son of _____, and advanced him and set his throne above all the officials who were with him.

What have we learned about the importance of names and genealogy? We have learned that when there is lineage present, we should pay attention.

Haman is listed as an Agagite.

Read 1 Samuel 15:1–9.

Did you find a familiar name? Agag was the king of the Amalekites.

So who were the Amalekites? Let's take a quick trip to Exodus 17:8–16.

The Amalekites were an ancient enemy of Israel. They attacked God's people as they exited Egypt, and God made a promise to remember what they had done and that He would "utterly blot out" their memory from the face of the earth.

However, in 1 Samuel, we see that King Saul has disobeyed God and King Agag was spared. The fact that Haman is listed as an "Agagite" tells us something. The original audience of this text would have known that the author intended for them to understand that Mordecai and Haman would be enemies—enemies who go back generations.[1]

There is another important detail to recognize.

WHAT DID THE KING COMMAND CONCERNING HAMAN (ESTHER 3:2)?

As a recipient of such a royal edict, it seems that this guy must have manipulated his way into power. Why else would a king have to demand, in law, for the servants of the realm to "bow down" and "pay homage"?

Have you ever felt like someone received something they did not deserve? Not only did they receive something they hadn't earned or had merit for, but something maybe you should have been given instead?

HOW DID YOU RESPOND?

A few years ago, I was passed over for a leadership position in a large nonprofit organization. Instead of being able to lead from the front, I was placed under the authority of someone I believed had not deserved the responsibility. She was new and green in team leadership, she had a rough attitude, and she really had (what I thought to be) a poor perspective toward serving others.

Nonetheless, God sovereignly placed her (and me) in the places He intended. I didn't respond well. I became resentful and frustrated, and ultimately, I left the organization sharply and with hard feelings. If it was a test from the Lord, I am 100 percent certain that I failed miserably.

So here's Mordecai, nearly five years after Esther had become queen (and after his heroic assassination intervention), seemingly passed over for promotion, disregarded, and unappreciated. I wonder how he felt. Did he feel like there had been an injustice? Was he frustrated? Angry?

HOW SHOULD WE RESPOND WHEN WE FEEL LIKE WE HAVE BEEN PASSED OVER?

The text doesn't say exactly how Mordecai felt, but we can see that he patiently endures.

Let's see what happens next.

WHAT DOES MORDECAI DO (ESTHER 3:2)?

The king's servants questioned Mordecai, asking why he would not comply. Even they were confused as to why he refused to honor and obey the king's command concerning Haman. They continued to urge him, speaking to him "day after day." This phrase, "day after day," is also used in Genesis, referencing Potiphar's wife pursuing Joseph. Genesis 39:10 says, "As she spoke to Joseph day after day, he would not listen to her." See the resemblance?

Some scholars believe that Mordecai does not bow out of pride or indignation. Others say it was because he was angry. I fall in the camp of those who believe he did not bow out of righteous anger and out of his need to stand for his belief in God. In those days, bowing was not simply an act of respect, like a courtesy or handshake, but was instead a form of worship.

IN ESTHER 3:4, WHAT DOES MORDECAI REVEAL ABOUT HIMSELF?

The fact that he explains his actions by revealing his identity as a Jew is bold. Up until this point, he has likely kept this particular piece of his identity hidden. It seems as though a line has been drawn in the sand.

WHAT ABOUT US? WHERE IS OUR "LINE IN THE SAND"? IS THERE A POINT WHERE YOU ARE WILLING TO STAND AND SAY NO TO THE DEMANDS AND DEBAUCHERY OF THIS WORLD, EVEN THOUGH IT MAY COST YOU SOMETHING?

Mordecai refuses to worship Haman and stands his ground. He patiently endures the perceived slight of being passed over. And finally, we watch as the battle begins to unfold between these two individuals.

But wait. Is the battle ever only between people? Is there an "us" and a "them"?

READ EPHESIANS 6:12 AND COPY IT HERE.

Does the buck stop with Haman or Mordecai? The Bible says it doesn't. Look at what you wrote above and underline what we do *not* wrestle with.

While Haman is an enemy, he is not *the* enemy. There is a real enemy who manipulates, lies, and steals. He is out to destroy what God has made and uses people to accomplish his goal.

However, about two thousand years ago, when Christ paid the cost for sin with His death and conquered death by the resurrection, the war was over. The enemy has lost forever. We can view these attacks and hard-fought battles of life differently. Even though it seems like we might be losing, ultimately, the victory has already been won.

How does the cross give you hope for the trials and tough times of today? Pray and reflect on how God's grace through Jesus gives us a new perspective in our own hardships and hurts.

WEEK 3 | DAY 2

READ ESTHER CHAPTER 3.

SCRIPTURE FOCUS: Esther 3:5–8

Today, we are going to uncover the beginnings of a conflict, a conflict that will set the stage for all that is to come in the rest of the book of Esther.

The king has issued an edict requiring all to bow before Haman. Mordecai has refused. Mordecai defied the king's order and is adamant in his stance. This refusal spurs Haman into rage. The Hebrew word used for "fury" is *chemah*. It means to be hot with rage, or in other contexts, it refers to vengeful wrath.[2]

We have a terrible tendency to whitewash the words of God and sometimes struggle to understand them as they were written. Hebrew is a poetic language, filled with strong verbs and intricate imagery. For example, we may read this verse and think, oh yes, I guess Haman was mad.

The original audience might have visualized it like this. "Upon Mordecai's refusal, Haman's blood boiled with contempt. His eyes grew fierce and he conjured a murderous look on his face. His anger blazed within him, foretelling his vengeful thoughts toward pain and suffering."

WHAT DID HAMAN SEEK TO DO?

Overreact much? In his anger, Haman "sought to destroy all the Jews" (v. 6) because they were the people of Mordecai. Let's remember, the Persian Empire was only slightly smaller than the entire United States. **Could you imagine the magnitude of seeking to eliminate an entire people group on such a grand scale?**

WHAT YEAR OF THE KING'S REIGN IS INDICATED IN THIS PASSAGE?

Yes, the story is now set in the twelfth year of Ahasuerus's reign. This epic tale began in his third year. Esther became queen in the seventh year. Somewhere in between Esther's crowning and Haman's advancement, Mordecai saved the king from assassination. Now, in the twelfth year, Haman is plotting destruction, or annihilation, of the Jews.

WHAT DOES HAMAN DO TO DETERMINE WHEN HE SHOULD ENACT HIS PLAN (SEE V. 7)?

So our boy Haman decides he is going to cast lots to determine when he should begin this plan of executing all of the Jews in the Persian Empire. What is a "lot" anyway? Well, "casting lots" was a way God's people in Old Testament times could determine His will. A "lot," or the Hebrew word *goral*, means a cube—like our modern-day dice—and connotes fate, destiny, and such.[3]

Unlike God's people, who sought direction from the Lord, the only living God, Haman was casting lots as some form of pagan divination.[4]

FIND PROVERBS 16:33 AND WRITE IT HERE.

Haman is rolling the dice to decide when God's people were to be wiped from the face of the earth, but his gods were not the authority on that decision.

WHO WAS SOVEREIGN, OR IN CHARGE, OF HOW THOSE "LOTS" FELL?

This is the point in the story where we begin to see the connections and intricacies between the things that happen to us, the things we suffer through, and some of the things we have chosen. **The beauty of this next passage is this: God can, and does, move faithfully through our circumstances, our longings, our sufferings, and our needs.**

WHEN DID THE "LOT" FALL?

Haman's lot landed in the month of Adar (March). This edict would be announced on Passover Eve. Cue Alanis again. "Isn't it ironic?"

This poses a pretty hard question. Would God remain faithful to His people, while they existed in exile? Would He remain faithful to His people even when His people had failed to be faithful to Him? We cannot know the hearts of every individual Jew living in exile. Certainly some had assimilated and were content enough to remain in Persia observing the ways of that culture. Other Jews loved God (Deuteronomy 6:5) and wanted to live for Him even in exile, even far from their promised land, even when the temple was gone. Others did not and remained in the indifference and rebellion that had gotten them exiled in the first place. The point here is *God's* faithfulness.

What do we think? Is He with us when we are outside of His will? Does His love hinge on our performance, or ability to be obedient? Is God still faithful to us, even when we are bearing the brunt of the consequences of our own sin or unfaithfulness?

The short answer? Absolutely. God is always with us. I hope as we journey through the rest of this study, the answer will become firmly planted in your heart.

All right, folks. It is time to take another deep breath and brace for impact. We are heading back into dark and sinister territory. Some of these places will move you to discomfort. Others will generate feelings of loss or mourning. Some of these places may cause you to be angry. Let's be committed to going (and staying) through together.

We pick up in verse 8, where Haman says to the king, "There is a certain people scattered abroad and dispersed among the peoples in all the provinces of your kingdom. Their laws are different from those of every other people, and they do not keep the king's laws, so that it is not to the king's profit to tolerate them."

What we are witnessing is the plotting and scheming that sparks the flame of genocide.

Haman sits down with the king to paint a picture of a dangerous, seditious people, a threat to the realm, and he presents a solution I can scarcely take in. He plays the role of being sympathetic to the king's interests—a tactic we have seen as successful before. He points out their separateness, that their ways are different, and the king's need to remove them.

We are watching blatant racism advance and evolve into a serious problem.

While we're studying this key part of the account of Esther, we can't help acknowledge that the stain of racism has been with humanity for eons. It was not new in Haman's time and it's not unknown in our own day. Racism takes many forms. Perhaps it's against a religious or ethnic group, such as Haman warning the king that "a certain people" in the empire cared nothing for his laws. It can be targeted against a skin tone. It can exist on a societal level or between individuals. Maybe there has been racism in your family that has been passed down for generations like an old heirloom. Maybe you yourself have experienced racism and the pain it causes. Possibly you have been a perpetrator of racism without even realizing it. Perhaps you are scratching your head and have no idea what I'm talking about.

Make no mistake, racism will be with us as long as we live in a fallen world. The enemy has been turning brother against brother and sister against sister from the beginning of time, and he doesn't seem likely to stop now.

The apostle Paul in Ephesians 2 provides an apt illustration of how, when we are in Christ, hostilities are broken down. He compares two groups: the Jews, who were the beneficiaries of the covenant of the promise; and those who are Gentiles (non-Jews) by birth. At one time, pious Jews did not understand that non-Jews could ever share in the promises, i.e., the promises of the coming Messiah. Paul explains, "He himself . . . has made the two groups one and has destroyed the barrier, the dividing wall of hostility. . . . His purpose was to create in himself one new humanity out of the two . . . to reconcile both of them to God through the cross" (Ephesians 2:14–16 NIV). We'll look at this passage again on day 4.

Every person who is in Christ is a part of Him. No barriers—of racism, social standing, education level, political preference, or anything at all—have any place in Christ's body, the church.

For some, the rest of this week may be difficult to wade through. We will be neck deep in the mud and mire of hate. We will have to look at what hate really costs us and what it costs those under the weight of it. We will not have the luxury of looking away. Death will be staring us in the face, smirking as we wriggle and writhe trying to shed our own guilt for harboring it.

If this sounds dark, don't quit now . . . for on the other side of this voyage is growth and love!

Take a moment and jot down a prayer. Ask God to open your heart and send His Spirit to show you what He has to say. Pray for steadfastness. What we do now is bold and courageous.

WEEK 3 | DAY 3

READ ESTHER CHAPTER 3.

SCRIPTURE FOCUS: Esther 3:9–11

The plot is being put into motion. Haman has cast the lot, and it has landed on the month of Adar—or March of our calendar. He approached the king for permission to execute his foul plan to eliminate an entire people group from the king's territories.

He began his pitch with five words—five words that seem to be an underlying theme throughout the book of Esther.

What five words begin in verse 9? "_____"

Haman is asking for multitudes of people to be destroyed.

I find it completely insane that the king is so easily manipulated that he agrees to the annihilation of an entire people group without Haman actually naming them. Haman says in verse 8 that "there is a certain people" the king should not concern himself with tolerating. He does not say "The Jews should not be tolerated."

Anti-Semitism—the hostility or prejudice against Jewish people—isn't a foreign concept to many of us. We grew up learning about Anne Frank, the Nazis, and the unfathomable death toll caused by the Holocaust. Now decades have passed since the atrocities of concentration camps, gas chambers, and mass communal graves, but these horrors are still remembered, as they should be.

The same kind of brutal and evil hate that spurred a Nazi regime to genocide sits inside the heart of Haman.

That is a lot of hate.

Do we tell ourselves we don't have this kind of malice, or do we pacify our own convictions of prejudice by measuring how "bad" our sin is in comparison?

I know I am beating this drum relatively hard, but we have got to stop wanting to identify one with the heroes of the Bible. We, as believers, sometimes have a bad habit of only recognizing our commonalities with people who are perceived as righteous or victorious.

God certainly speaks through story, specifically in His Word—the story of Himself, His people, and His plan for salvation in Jesus. But we cannot cut and snip away at these other stories—stories meant to teach and instruct us—in order to puff up pride, tout our ability to follow rules, or deny ourselves as sinners. We have to acknowledge that there are dark rooms in the halls of our hearts we would rather keep closed or hidden. Some of the darkest rooms may hold feelings of hate, of prejudice, or even of supremacy.

I grew up in the deep South. Louisiana was my childhood home and later our family relocated to Texas. The South has some of my most favorite things—fried food, breakfast tacos, and small-town community. But it is also home to deep-seated racism and hotbeds of hate.

There was and still is most certainly a racial divide.

WHAT ABOUT WHERE YOU GREW UP? WAS THERE RACIAL TENSION?

LOOKING BACK, DID YOU FEEL LIKE RACISM WAS JUST AN ACCEPTED PART OF
LIFE? OR IS THIS CONCEPT COMPLETELY FOREIGN?

Take a moment to reflect because, as we press on through the rest of this week, we
are going to have to come face to face with our own hearts. For now, let's go back
to the text.

HOW MUCH DOES HAMAN OFFER TO PAY TO THE KING'S TREASURIES?

This would have been an outrageous sum. Herodotus, our favorite secular Greek
historian, estimates the king's annual revenue to have been around 15,000 talents
of silver.[5] Haman is offering nearly 60 percent of the annual empire earnings.
Maybe Haman was trying to persuade the king, not only with emotional
manipulation, but encouragement that his treasuries would not be depleted in the
mass killing of his subjects.

I don't want us to miss this. This is not just another day at the office where a vice
president and CEO are discussing best business practices and productivity cuts.
People's lives are at stake. We are talking about blatant and unapologetic genocide.

WHAT DID THE KING GIVE TO HAMAN?

By this gesture, the king is granting Haman royal authority to do as he pleases.
This decree would be drafted and be signed, then sealed with the king's royal
signet, signifying the king's authoritative will.

WHAT NEW TITLE, OR DESIGNATION, IS GIVEN TO HAMAN BY THE AUTHOR OF
ESTHER IN VERSE 10?

Pretty clear, isn't it? If we were confused about Haman's position or place in the story of Esther, the author has just made it perfectly clear. This is a bad dude and he has his sight on destruction.

Then, the last section of this passage, verse 11, says, "And the king said to Haman, 'The money is given to you, the people also, to do with them as it seems good to you.'"

I can hardly type the verse without a cold chill running down my spine.

It would seem, at this moment, that the enemy was winning.

We haven't seen the whole picture yet, but if this scene were in a movie, the camera lenses would be zero focused in on the two evil men who had just sealed the fate of God's people. We would begin to sweat, wondering if God would show up in time.

While we let the suspense hang in the air until tomorrow, let's spend the rest of our time reflecting on the person of Haman.

FIND PROVERBS 6:16–19 AND WRITE OUT WHAT THE LORD HATES.

Do you think there is something to be said about the behavior of this man?

A friend and mentor, Jill Briscoe, taught me something about reading Scripture. She said, "Dear, when I read God's Word, I always look for a promise to claim, a warning to heed, a command to obey, something about Jesus, and something about me."

So what about us? Do we actively defend our right to any of these abominable sins? Do we explain or excuse them away with phrases like "It was just how I was raised" or "I'm not as bad as _____." Is there a warning to heed here?

Take a moment to confess and reflect in prayer. Ask God to shine a light on what He would have you see. May He give you peace as you search, spur you forward to lean on Him, and help us as we unpack more and more about His character.

WEEK 3 | DAY 4

READ ESTHER CHAPTER 3.

SCRIPTURE FOCUS: Esther 3:11

"And the king said to Haman, 'The money is given to you, the people also, to do with them as it seems good to you.'"

Yesterday, we began to scratch the surface on the hate displayed in racism. We began the uneasy task of searching our own hearts to reveal how we deal with prejudice and preference. Today we will dig deeper still.

In venturing through the book of Esther, verse by verse, we let the text determine the topics we will learn about.

Ultimately, Esther has several recurring themes: God's sovereignty (His authority) over all circumstances, God's provision (His goodness in providing for the needs of His children), and God's faithfulness (His commitment to do what He says He will do).

This book also touches on topics relevant for us today. Racism is one of those topics, and we would do well to lean in a little further to reflect.

A few years ago, I attended a luncheon for women of color during a large women's conference. I wasn't sure what to expect, but I was eager to attend. The event was coordinated by and for women of color in the Christian sphere. At an event with nearly four thousand women in Dallas, Texas, the women of color luncheon could fit inside a humble movie theater. I looked around at the other 115 or so fiercely bold women and I was overcome with emotion.

At the time, I was thirty-two and had not yet let myself identify as a woman of color. My biological father immigrated to the United States from Thailand in the early eighties, but was absent in my life. Since he left before I was born, though I was half Thai and half white, I never allowed myself to explore my Asian ethnicity. Mostly because, growing up in the deep South, my ethnicity was little more than a reason to be mocked or ridiculed. This luncheon would change everything for me.

When I sat down in the theater chair, gospel worship music flowed from the speakers. Women, in unity, began to sing. Then Latasha Morrison, the founder of the Be the Bridge organization, began to speak and ask questions. It was nothing short of transformative.

"What is it like to be a woman of color in the church?" The question exploded into the air as if someone had just politely lobbed a hand grenade into our midst. The responses from the women in the room were earthshakingly freeing. All of a sudden, I wasn't alone in my struggle. Others too had felt overlooked, ignored, and suffered through being made to feel "less than."

We came together to pray over one another. I sat down next to Maria, who asked me to pray for reformation to come to Latin America. I listened as Native American women voiced their experiences in the church. Women led from the stage, praying in English, Mandarin Chinese, Spanish, and Swahili. I believe the gathering in that room was absolutely kindred to the early church—a feeling I have longed to re-experience ever since.

FIND REVELATION 7:9–12. EITHER COPY THIS PASSAGE OR SUMMARIZE IT HERE.

This is a picture of heaven—what it will be like in the courts of His throne. This passage tells us something important. We will retain our ethnicity in heaven. I will stand, as an Asian woman, in the courts of my King, dressed in white robes, with a palm branch in my hand.

We will all be there together, crying out, "Salvation belongs to our God who sits on the throne, and to the Lamb!"

Revelation 7 is telling us there is no division in heaven.

What about here on earth? Can we abide any sort of racism here?

FIND AND READ EPHESIANS 2:11–22.

Paul is writing to the church in Ephesus. In this letter, he is taking a good look at how to live out what we believe in Christ Jesus as His followers. In this chapter, he is sharing how we are saved, by grace through faith (v. 8), and then imparting to us the unity in Christ's own blood.

READ EPHESIANS 2:14–16. WHAT DOES THE TEXT SAY HE (JESUS) CREATED?

What do you think Paul, who wrote this letter, means by "one new man in place of two"? This particular passage is talking about the reconciliation of the two peoples—Jews and Gentiles. We have said before that the Jews of that time referred to non-Jews as Gentiles.

Because of the cross, the two, Jews and Gentiles, have been reconciled into one new person—in Christ. These two passages, and many others, confirm that racism is not the will of God, nor should we subscribe to any version of Christianity that brands hate in God's name.

Let's examine ourselves honestly. Have we misunderstood the gospel? Is there an "us" and a "them" in our mind?

We have got to move away from the mentality that racism is just part of our reality and reframe our thoughts to drive us to be the solution. The church should be leading the way in the reduction of racism in our world, but where do we start? Latasha Morrison's Be the Bridge groups outline nine steps toward racial reconciliation and healing. We will talk about two; awareness and the process of acknowledgment and lament.[6]

First, we have to become aware of the problem. We have to marry our intentions with action and begin to educate ourselves about racism in our society, our communities, and inside our own hearts. A great resource is the Be the Bridge Facebook group. There you'll find a ton of media and content centered around how to begin to understand the problem of racism. Another pivotal resource I discovered was the Acts 29 "Racial Reconciliation" panel on Vimeo. I watched Eyes on the Prize, a documentary series on the civil rights movement, along with the PBS series Many Rivers to Cross. These things opened my eyes.

WHAT WILL YOU COMMIT TO RESEARCHING OR LEARNING IN THIS SEASON?

Next, we should pursue acknowledgment and lament. Morrison writes, "Forgiveness and healing cannot begin until we become aware of the historical roots of the problem and acknowledge the harm caused."[7] These broken systems and racial tension lines should cause us to lament—to grieve—over the state of our world.

Are you grieved by the open wounds and hurts many of our peers face daily? Jot down a prayer for those in pain, and for the Lord to allow you to grieve alongside them.

Racism is not just a problem for people of color. It is incumbent for all of us, as believers, to communally stand against hate and discrimination.

In Esther's time, the hate hidden in Haman's heart manifested as a scheme to blot an unimaginable number of people from the vast empire. His hate consumed him and, ultimately, it will bring him to his end.

If we can learn anything from this week's passages and the ones to come, it is that God opposes the proud—and attitudes such as racism and xenophobia (fear or hatred of the foreign) are rooted in pride and superiority.

Be encouraged, this work is hard, and sometimes uncomfortable, but God brings growth and fresh understanding. We can lean in to uncomfortable topics together, knowing that the God of all grace is calling us forward.

Take a moment to jot down any thoughts or prayers from today's homework.

WEEK 3 | DAY 5

READ ESTHER CHAPTER 3.

SCRIPTURE FOCUS: Esther 3:9–15

Let's get a recap of the events in Esther's third chapter. Haman the Agagite is promoted, and all the king's subjects are ordered to pay homage to him. Mordecai the Jew, Esther's cousin, refuses, sending Haman into a fiery rage. Haman begins to plot, scheming to coldheartedly wipe the Jewish people from the face of the empire.

In preparation, Haman begins in the month of Nisan (March) to cast "Pur," or throw dice, to determine in which month he shall strive to commit blatant and unapologetic genocide. He does this and finally arrives at a date—a date he believes is determined by his gods. The date decided on to eliminate the Jewish people would correspond on our calendar to February/March, nearly a year later.

"Isn't it ironic?" It's ironic that in the month God's people are preparing to celebrate Passover—the time of feasts and remembrance of God's deliverance of the Israelites from slavery in Egypt—they would instead be presented with a mass death warrant.

As a mother of four young children, I am often reminded of my lack of ability to be consistent or follow through with what I promise. I make my best attempt at scolding or redirecting, often adding the possibility of consequence or reward. "If you will behave, and do what I tell you, we can do something fun after I'm finished working." Or "I promise we'll get ice cream if you can be quiet during my phone call" (it almost never works). But I find that I can't always follow through with what I have committed to.

Luckily for us, God is not an overwhelmed or exhausted parent. He always follows through with what He promises.

When the announcement was proclaimed throughout the kingdom of Ahasuerus, I'm sure there was one question running through the minds of God's people. "Will God deliver us?"

They were living outside of God's promised land, unable to experience the fullness of the Jewish way of life as they had in the promised land, with God and His worship at the center. Could and would God move in a foreign place? Would God intervene on behalf of His people, even those in Persia? They were far from the temple, which had been destroyed anyway. Is God really in charge here?

Let's bring these questions into our time.

IS GOD'S WILLINGNESS TO SAVE BASED ON OUR PERFORMANCE?

When I became a believer, I was still steeped in the idea that I had to earn God's love. Everything hinged on my ability to showcase a righteous life, attend church every week, and model the highest qualities of what I understood to be biblical womanhood. Only then, did I believe God could love me.

How wrong I was.

Does God desire my life to reflect the fruits of righteousness? Yes. Does He want me to spend time in worship with brothers and sisters in the faith? Yes. Is there instruction on how to live for His glory as a woman? Sure. But these are not the reasons I am able to be loved by God. I, and you, can know we are loved by God because of the work on the cross of Christ. In that moment, when Jesus voluntarily laid down His life and took it up again, we were made clean, reconciled to God, and justified. Christ took our punishment. He paid for our sins. He did this because we are loved—*and for no other reason.*

You see, God's people had not performed, or "held up their end." Those in exile in Persia were living away from God's promised land. They had been exiled from it because of disobedience to His law, which included not allowing any idolatry to seep into their lives or land, and now they were wondering if God had forsaken or given up on them. For the Jews, God had entered into a covenant, a promise, with them and He is faithful.

But Haman wasted no time after his permission from the king. He had manipulated King Ahasuerus into consenting to genocide. Haman immediately activated the scribes and ordered them to issue the edict of destruction.

WHAT DID THE EDICT ORDER (ESTHER 3:13)?

The message was clear. Kill everyone and take their belongings. The letters were sent by couriers throughout the Persian Empire directing that in a little less than a year's time, all of Persia should rise up to erase the Jewish people from history.

It is important to note the immense tragedy taking place here. In one afternoon, two leaders have just sanctioned the mass murder and eradication of an entire people group. Afterward, they sit down to a "drink" while "the city of Susa was thrown into confusion." They were thrown into confusion because their leader was capable of malevolent genocide. He was weak in character and easily malleable. **Could any good come from such a fool-hearted and nefarious reign?**

Haman's success is complete. He maneuvered the king into accomplishing his will. The signet ring is his. His desire to wipe God's people from the face of the earth seems to be realized.

Where is God?

People have grappled with the question of the *whys* of good and evil and the goodness of God since the beginning of time. For our purposes in studying the book of Esther, we won't dive deep into these things other than to say that as Christians, we believe in God's providence.

What is providence? While you won't find this word in the Bible, the principle is threaded all through the story of Scripture. God is in charge and He provides. Biblical providence holds that God is the Creator and the Sustainer of all things, and nothing is outside His control. This is providence.

One tool to help us better understand God's providence is the Heidelberg Catechism. A catechism is a summary of Christian beliefs, formatted by presenting questions and answers. For hundreds of years, many Christians have memorized the questions and answers in order to understand what they believed and why.

The Heidelberg Catechism addresses God's providence in the twenty-seventh and twenty-eighth questions.[8] They read:

27. Q. What do you understand by the providence of God?

   A. Providence is the almighty and ever present power of God by which He upholds, as with His hand, heaven and earth and all creatures, and so rules them that leaf and blade, rain and drought, fruitful and lean years, food and drink, health and sickness, prosperity and poverty—all things, in fact, come to us not by chance but from His fatherly hand.

28. Q. How does the knowledge of God's creation and providence help us?

   A. We can be patient when things go against us, thankful when things go well, and for the future we can have good confidence in our faithful God and Father that nothing will separate us from His love. All creatures are so completely in His hand that without His will they can neither move or be moved. So how can we, when things appear bleak or we are faced with hard circumstances, still trust that God is good?

We can strive to know what we believe about Him and why we believe it.

Find Psalm 105 in your Bible and read through it.

LET'S FOCUS ON VERSE 8. WRITE IT HERE.

What does God remember forever? He remembers His covenant—His promises.

Back to Esther 3. Here we find God's people and the city of Susa facing the eradication of an entire people group. Will God show up or let them fall?

The Hebrew word for "confusion" is *nabokah*.[9] It means to aimlessly wander. They were overtaken with such disbelief and were uneasy about seeing what the future held. They were heartbroken by the decree and wrestling with doubt.

Simultaneously, we see Haman and the king sitting down to eat and drink. The callousness of their hearts makes me grieve. Their immense indifference to the sting of death is chilling.

But before we turn our noses up in contempt, we need to check ourselves and our hearts.

As we are sitting comfortably in our homes with a cracked Bible, a hot mug of coffee, and a pen scribbling away in this workbook, billions of men and women are feeling around in the dark. They are lost and looking for answers.

We have the answer in Christ Jesus, but we are slow to mobilize toward His command in the Great Commission—the command to share the gospel *and* make disciples. We can be just as indifferent to the spiritual death that the world is experiencing as Haman and King Ahasuerus.

Sara Barratt, the author of *Love Riot*, said something profound during an interview for *Military Spouse* magazine. She said we have to "reject the apathy that suggests that discipleship is someone else's job."[10]

People outside of Christ are most certainly still dead in their sin. They have not heard the freeing message of the gospel, but they are not forgotten. God is in fierce pursuit, calling all of His children to participate in heralding a message of hope—the hope of Christ.

HOW ARE YOU TAKING AN ACTIVE PART IN SHARING THE REDEMPTIVE STORY OF JESUS IN YOUR LOCAL CHURCH AND COMMUNITY?

As God's people in Susa and beyond began the task of facing a terrifying ordeal, little did they know that God already had a plan. He had already begun moving behind the scenes to orchestrate His great providence. Esther and Mordecai have been perfectly positioned for His purposes.

Jesus, in Matthew 9, teaches us a good thing to pray for is more "workers"—for gospel carriers. Take a moment to jot down a prayer asking God to raise up more gospel communicators, teachers, and disciple makers. Ask Him also to let it begin with you.

SUMMONED

to Share Sorrow

WEEK 4 | DAY 1

READ ESTHER CHAPTER 4.

SCRIPTURE FOCUS: Esther 4:1–3

Lament. Lamenting isn't something we hear about often in today's Christian culture. Merriam Webster defines lament as "to mourn aloud" or "to express sorrow, mourning, or regret for, often demonstratively."[1] Basically, it means to lay bare our emotions before God, to deeply express our pain to Him who is faithful.

WHAT DID MORDECAI DO WHEN WE HEARD THE NEWS OF THE DECREE?

Mordecai was an official of the court. He would have found out about this edict swiftly. This passage is describing Mordecai's prompt and immediate response to Haman's death decree for all Jewish people in the Persian realm.

WHAT WAS THE RESPONSE "IN EVERY PROVINCE . . . AMONG THE JEWS"?

Sackcloth was a rough and itchy garment primarily made from goat's hair. It was coarse and irritating to wear. It was used by the Israelites to show repentance, mourning, and grief.

Genesis 37:34 mentions sackcloth when Jacob puts the garment on to mourn the loss of his son. Psalm 30:11 also mentions sackcloth being removed by God and mourning replaced with joy. Ashes also are a reference to grief. The *Zondervan Illustrated Bible Dictionary* explains that the wearing of ashes "contrasts the lowliness of mortals with the dignity of God."[2]

Wearing sackcloth and sitting in ashes was a God-honoring way to express sorrow and pain—lament.

On hearing the news that all Jews, young and old, women and children, were to be destroyed at the hands of Haman, Mordecai fell into sadness. He tore his clothes and wept bitterly.

When we read through the accounts of God's people in Scripture, it is important to recognize that these narratives, or stories, are recorded reports of what happened. They may not necessarily have the intent to teach a specific principle or instruct us to copy the characters' behavior in the story. However, many times, we can glean certain themes from the text.

For example, in this passage, we can observe an appropriate and biblical response to pain and suffering.

WHAT ARE SOME THINGS IN OUR WORLD WE CAN LAMENT? WHAT ARE SOME WAYS WE CAN EXPRESS PAIN AND SUFFERING BEFORE GOD?

Because I am half Thai and half white, I have always been keenly aware that I was different. When I was younger, it was the fact that my tan skin and pitch-black hair stood out.

When I was a little older, it was the racist jokes at my expense that painfully stung me and caused me to be uncomfortable in larger crowds of my peers. Journeying through my teenage years, the sneers and disgusting innuendos from distasteful men also confirmed my separateness.

As an adult, I am still grappling with what it means to be a woman of color and how this specific descriptor impacts every aspect of my life.

Watching the horrific events that have happened over the last several years because of racial tensions and tragedy, I lament. My heart hurts over the contents of my social media feed, the internet videos showcasing pain and suffering, and a culture that so often sidesteps the hard work toward real change.

As a woman of color, I cry out before the Lord to heal these hurts, or give me the endurance and perseverance needed to sustain my joy in the midst of the wounds.

One way I work through my lament is by seeking out the truth in God's Word— trusting that God has something to say. Even while I grapple with hard feelings and tough thoughts, God's Word offers truth and comfort.

Find Joel 1:13–15.

DID YOU NOTICE ANY FAMILIAR WORDING OR PHRASES? WRITE THEM HERE.

Joel was a minor prophet, and the book that bears his name is estimated by some scholars to be written somewhere between 609–586 BC, nearly a hundred years before Ahasuerus's reign. ("Minor" prophet means that the books in the Bible named after these prophets are shorter than the longer books in that genre.)

Why is this important? It seems as if the author of Esther is alluding to the phrasing held in Joel. The Bible is often written in familiar language so readers and hearers would gain better insight into the author's intent.

Let's look a little further. Find Joel 2:12–14.

"Yet even now," declares the LORD, "return to me with all your heart . . ." What an encouragement. How clearly can we hear the themes held in Joel nestled here in Esther.

WRITE OR SUMMARIZE JOEL 2:14 HERE.

"Who knows . . . ?" This question is presenting God's sovereignty. John Piper defines sovereignty as God's "right and power to do all that he decides to do."[3] Essentially, God is in charge and He will do whatever He decides to do, when He decides to do it.

DO YOU THINK MORDECAI BELIEVED GOD WAS IN CHARGE OF THIS SITUATION? WHAT CLUES IN THE PASSAGE CAN YOU FIND THAT HELPED YOU ANSWER?

Take a moment to reflect on how you can learn from the story in Esther. Think about how we can position our hearts and trust His provision during hard times. Pray and ask God to help you lean into His grace and mercy.

WEEK 4 | DAY 2

READ ESTHER CHAPTER 4.

SCRIPTURE FOCUS: Esther 4:4–8

We left off yesterday with Mordecai weeping and mourning over the gut-wrenching news of pending destruction. Today, we will see how Esther responds.

HOW DID ESTHER FEEL IN RESPONSE TO LEARNING OF MORDECAI'S MOURNING (ESTHER 4:4)?

Esther quickly mobilized to provide garments for Mordecai. We learned from the first few verses in chapter 4 that it was illegal to enter the king's gate when in sackcloth. These kings of old did not like the sadness and sufferings of the real world to be permitted within their gates. So the presence of people mourning and weeping would have ruined the king's merry attitude, and that could not be permitted.

Esther, attempting to fix the situation, sends her cousin new clothes to get him out of sackcloth.

There is a bad habit we have as believers. We don't like seeing people in pain and, because it makes us uncomfortable, we storm in to save the day before we know what is actually wrong.

I remember once when I was still new to being in a Bible study group, a woman in the room started to cry. She was bravely and vulnerably sharing a hard story with those of us who were present. One of the problems she was battling was the difficulty of being an active duty military family. She was lonely, and her frustrations of being away from home were mounting. She was looking to us in the group for reassurance and encouragement.

Immediately, the study facilitator started offering solutions (unsolicited advice) and giving instructions on how to fix her problems. This well-intentioned leader suggested that the troubled woman attend a few spouses' functions or try counseling. Looking back, I realize that the leader meant well, but was overly quick to advise rather than actively listen. She was offering solutions before hearing the woman fully express herself. I have tried to remember this event as a lesson to me when I'm in the position of being the teacher.

Don't get me wrong. I'm not busting Esther for being insensitive, nor do I think the text is specifically saying that she was. I am, however, convicted by the manner in which she quickly tries to rush in and fix things before finding out what the problem actually entails. We need to have the mindset of serving people rather than fixing their situation.

HAVE THERE BEEN TIMES YOU RUSHED IN TO FIX A PROBLEM BEFORE HAVING ALL THE DETAILS? HOW DID THAT WORK OUT?

When we jump in to solve problems from a half-baked perspective, we run the risk of missing the mark entirely. We need to commit ourselves to digging deeper with people and asking the right questions.

Mordecai is lamenting, crying out before the Lord, and in great pain. This passage also shows us that we do not have to "think good thoughts" and accept the narrative that Christians are always happy or positive.

Scholar and author Walter Kaiser says, "God has placed personal and national laments in Scripture, it would appear, as a corrective against euphoric, celebratory notions of faith, which romantically portray life as consisting only of sweetness and light. . . . God has given us in the laments of Scripture a solace where the full spectrum of our earthly journey can be represented."[4]

We should reject the notion that being a believer in Jesus requires us to slap on a smile and pretend that everything is all good. The Scriptures, such as in Lamentations and the Psalms among other places, walk us through the entire spectrum of human emotions. **God does not want our false positivity or platitudes. Instead, He offers us an authentic relationship—one where we can come before Him just as we are—with our brokenness, anger, and hurt in tow.**

WHY DO YOU THINK ESTHER SENT MORDECAI GARMENTS?

Esther most likely sent Mordecai clothing in order to make it possible for him to enter into the king's gate. He was probably making quite a spectacle, and Esther may have wanted him to stop drawing attention to himself. Assuming that she had all the answers, she sent Mordecai what she believed would solve his problem.

WHAT DID ESTHER DO NEXT (ESTHER 4:5)?

When I think about guys like Hathach, obscure people within the stories of Scripture, I am deeply encouraged. Hathach had a huge responsibility and an integral role in the unfolding events of this story—all the while unbeknownst to him and to others.

What about us? Do we recognize that we too have integral roles in God's story today? We can be intentionally observing where God is working and choose to join Him there. We can lean into the wisdom held within His Word and be obedient in following His will through the power of the Holy Spirit.

So Hathach approaches Mordecai and a verbal exchange takes place.

WHAT DID MORDECAI TELL HATHACH AND WHAT DID HE GIVE HIM?

This exchange confirms that Mordecai had a higher position within the Persian court.[5]

Because Esther was separated and in the seclusion of the royal harem, she would not have heard the news of Haman's death decree. In addition, up until this point she has been intentionally hiding her identity as a Jewish woman. Maybe no one thought she would need to know, as it would not have affected her.

WHAT DID MORDECAI TELL HATHACH TO "COMMAND" OF ESTHER ON HIS BEHALF (ESTHER 4:8)?

Mordecai implores Esther to act. Earlier in the book of Esther, Mordecai had "commanded" Esther to keep her identity as a Jewish woman hidden. And she obeyed. But, now, the time for hiding has ended. Lives are at stake.

This will be the turning point in the book of Esther. What will happen? Will Esther respond and rush to the aid of her people? Or will she find an excuse or make it someone else's problem?

As we continue to explore through this chapter of Esther, we should know that God offers us many opportunities to work alongside Him, to be active participants in His sovereign plans. We have to decide if we are going to willingly obey and act; or will we let these chances pass us by?

Jot down a prayer, asking God to make you aware of His calling and to help you focus on hearing His will through His Word.

WEEK 4 | DAY 3

READ ESTHER CHAPTER 4.

SCRIPTURE FOCUS: Esther 4:9–11

Have you ever watched a debate, with arguments and presentations being lobbed back and forth? In my mind, this conversation in Esther feels like watching an intense tennis match, with reasons and excuses being served back and forth with great speed.

Mordecai had been sitting in sackcloth and ashes. Esther sends brighter garments for him to change into. He rejects the offering. Confused, Esther sends her royal appointed eunuch, Hathach, to find out what is happening. Mordecai tells him everything, down to the dollar amount Haman is paying the king to destroy the entire Jewish population. Mordecai also implores Hathach to command Esther to intervene on behalf of their people.

After all this, Esther sends Hathach back to Mordecai with a response.

HOW DOES ESTHER RESPOND? DOES IT SOUND LIKE ESTHER WANTS TO HEED MORDECAI'S PLEA FOR HELP?

Esther begins with a simple lesson in the law of the land of Persia, which is this: Come before the king unsummoned and be put to death. Death was certain unless the king himself lowered his golden scepter as a sign of approval and warm welcome.

It was customary for those seeking an audience with the king to send a message through his official chain of communication—his eunuchs. Then, if the king wished to see the person requesting a meeting, he would summon them to court.

Esther is leery of crashing in unannounced because it would put her in danger, and the king was unpredictable. Do you remember the beginning of the book of Esther? Vashti, who broke the law by refusing the king, was banished. Adios, outta here, don't let the door hit ya on your way out.

So Esther naturally does not want to show up uninvited for fear of execution. Simultaneously, she provides another excuse as to why she should not do what Mordecai has asked.

HOW LONG HAD IT BEEN SINCE THE KING HAD SUMMONED HER (SEE 4:11)?

Esther is indicating to Mordecai that the king may be losing interest in her. I mean, we know this guy was not lonely or going to sleep in an empty bed. Perhaps Esther had fallen from favor.

Conceivably, she is telling Mordecai that her death would be certain if she went into the king without going through the proper channels because he had already tired of her. Now, five years into their marriage, Esther has not been summoned for an entire month to spend the night with the king.

We don't know all that was in Esther's heart and mind. It sounds here that she is more concerned with her own safety than the safety of her kinsmen, the Jews. Have you heard the saying "Those in glass houses should not throw stones"? I have no intention of rock slinging at our girl Esther. I, too, live in a glass house at times.

You see, my issue is not hesitation when I believe I am called to act. Instead, my problem is that I say yes to far too many things while rarely considering the consequences of taking on another responsibility.

One day, while speaking with a friend, she made the keen observation that I tend to quickly overload my proverbial plate with far too many obligations, get subsequently overwhelmed, throw everything off by quitting or saying no, and then repeat the cycle all over again.

WHAT ABOUT YOU? WHEN IT COMES TO ACCEPTING GOD'S INVITATION TO MOVE, DO YOU TAKE ON FAR TOO MUCH, OR NOT ENOUGH?

There are two concepts we should examine in this chapter. **First, God has a sovereign purpose He is working toward. Second, He uses ordinary people like you and me to accomplish it.**

We can see that, in and through the story of Esther, God has been moving. He has a purpose He is always moving toward. In Esther's day, it was the rescue of His people and solidifying their place in the future.

He also has a purpose He is working toward today. In addition, His purpose today involves us. We have a role to play in the plan of a sovereign God. All we need to do is make the decision.

IS THERE SOMETHING YOU BELIEVE GOD HAS CALLED YOU TO DO?

I remember having a conversation with a pastor from my home church a few years ago. We were discussing the idea of living with purpose. The phrase "living with purpose," or "walking out your purpose," is one that I hear often in women's ministry.

I was frustrated because church people, particularly women, were obsessed with "finding *their* purpose." Women would constantly struggle with what God was calling them to do or be. They would spend hours scouring self-help books or listening to podcasts by women who apparently had figured it out.

He said something that helped me clarify how to respond to these women who were steeped in concepts like destiny. He said, "God rarely reveals His unknown will to those who are not already walking in His known will."

Here is what I'm trying to say. When we are more concerned with finding *our* purpose, not finding God's purposes, we will always miss the mark. God has given us His Word, a revelation of Himself, His will, and His ways. The Bible is our answer book, specifically our answer to the question of *What does God want me to do?* He calls us to know Him, love Him, and share Him.

IS THERE SOMETHING YOU KNOW GOD WANTS YOU TO DO THAT YOU JUST HAVEN'T BEEN ABLE TO?

I was talking with a woman who had regularly attended our weekly Bible study. As we were drinking coffee and talking about different aspects of life, she blurted out, "I wish God would just tell me what He wants me to do!" She was discouraged. She had grown up in the church and spent her life around people who seemed to have it all together, and the primary focus in her life was her inability to "live up to her purpose."

I'm going to ask you the same questions I asked her.

Are you part of a local church?

Are you in His Word regularly, spending quality time with Him?

If you are married, do you understand the call to biblical marriage, seeking to serve with and alongside your spouse?

If you are a parent, are you willingly shepherding your children?

Is there a sense of urgency in your life when it comes to sharing the redemptive story of Jesus?

These are all things that we know God is calling us to do. We should be active members, living and breathing parts, of a local church. We should prioritize our time to sit at the feet of our God, listening intently to hear Him speak through His Word. Our hearts should be fixed on our spouses, understanding that marriage is an institution that gives God glory. And we should be striving to raise our children to know and love the Lord. Likewise, we know that it is the calling of every believer to be and make disciples. Rather than making God fit into our plans, we should figure out how we fit into His plans.

So many times, we beg God for opportunities to serve Him in ways that cater to our own self-importance. We want to write bestsellers or speak on a stage before the multitudes, but we haven't even begun to walk within His known will for each of us. The point of asking all these questions is not to overwhelm or bring shame, but to put in right perspective the heart of God. He is already giving us many opportunities to serve Him in our daily lives. Have we answered His invitation?

In Esther's case, she is being given the opportunity to serve God in a big way, by taking her own life into her hands. She is being summoned by a heavenly King to go unsummoned before an earthly one.

Is this truly the kind of opportunity we would want to ask God for?

The message in this Bible study is not "Be brave like Esther" or "Be the queen God meant you to be."

Rather, this Bible study is an ardent call for us to examine our own hearts and find that we, like the characters in Scripture are, more often than not, self-centered and self-focused.

Esther was consumed by the thought that her intervention may lead to her immediate demise and, like many of us if faced with the same scenario, she hesitated to move.

HOW CAN YOU BE WALKING IN GOD'S KNOWN WILL THIS WEEK?

WHAT IS ONE AREA WHERE YOU WILL BE MORE COMMITTED TO FOCUSING?

DO YOU ANTICIPATE ANY OBSTACLES IN RESPONDING TO GOD IN THIS WAY? WRITE THEM HERE.

Take a moment to pray over this area in your life, asking God to bless it or grow it. Ask Him to walk with you as you seek His will.

WEEK 4 | DAY 4

READ ESTHER CHAPTER 4.

SCRIPTURE FOCUS: Esther 4:12–14

At the beginning of this week's study, we watched Mordecai become utterly inconsolable at the news decreed and issued by Haman. Destruction was coming, and Mordecai wept bitterly in sackcloth. Esther, attempting to comfort him and cease his public display of lament, sent him replacement clothing. After he rejected her gift, she begins to communicate with him via her king's appointed eunuch, Hathach. They begin lobbing logic and excuses back and forth like a game of badminton, and today we will examine Mordecai's response. In these two brief lines of Scripture, we will find deep encouragement and rich theological truths.

Some commentaries have said that Mordecai's response rings of an issued threat, that he had the intention of revealing her identity and betraying her to the king if she did not act on behalf of the Jews.

However, I do not believe that this is the case.

In researching this particular exchange, it seems to me that this is a loving exhortation between Mordecai and Esther. He is not afraid to say hard things or point to hard truths.

Many years ago, I was leading a moms' ministry on the Gulf Coast. What had started as a small group meeting in our family living room exploded into a full-blown ministry program. After partnering with our local Air Force chapel, a team of ministry military spouses and I were leading ten simultaneous Bible studies and coordinating a children's ministry with over a hundred kids.

I was still very green in leadership, and very self-confident. One could even use the word "arrogant." I was so passionate for the mission and so goal-oriented that I sometimes ignored my team's advice, or even failed to ask for it in the first place.

During a team meeting, I announced an all-new ministry plan and rollout agenda for the following year. I had come up with it entirely on my own, and I was beyond proud. I had worked out all the logistics, the annual theme, and completely changed some of our tried and true methods.

Another military spouse who was leading alongside me spoke up rather abruptly. In love, she openly corrected my selfish thinking. She said, "This is wrong and not how we should be operating. You can't just cut everyone out because you think you have all the answers. We have to do this together." It was convicting. In blazing through everyone else's lane in leadership, I had completely subverted the team's input, not even offering anyone else the chance to contribute.

Sometimes we, or those in our intimate circles, have to say hard truths.

WHAT DOES MORDECAI SAY TO ESTHER IN VERSE 13?

FIND PROVERBS 27:6 AND WRITE IT HERE.

Do you have a friend or family member who does not shy away from the hard task of "calling you on the carpet" or holding you accountable? Are you the type of friend who would lovingly approach another in the hopes of pointing them toward Jesus in their beliefs or behavior?

If I close my eyes, I can hear the concern and urgency in his voice as he exhorts Esther to take a personal inventory and to act.

He says a hard thing: Don't think your royal status or queenly residence will save you.

He is diligent in pointing out that the human things she would cling to, like royal security or hidden identity, would not be enough to keep her out of harm's way.

WHAT DOES MORDECAI SAY WILL HAPPEN IF ESTHER DOES NOT INTERVENE (V. 14)?

Have you ever heard the word "workaround"? As a military spouse, I am a master of the "workaround." Because of changing operational tempo, wonky schedules, and insane stress levels, I am constantly finding ways to achieve my desired outcomes without using the initial method I had intended. Workarounds are part of my daily life. In this section, Mordecai is referring to God's ability to work around us.

A. W. Tozer, in *The Knowledge of the Holy*, uses the illustration of an enormous ocean liner traveling from England to America. The people on board are free to do whatever they want to while they are on the journey, but they can't change the direction or course of the boat.

He writes, "The mighty liner of God's sovereign design keeps its steady course over the sea of history. God moves undisturbed and unhindered toward the fulfillment of those eternal purposes which He purposed in Christ Jesus before the world began."[6]

This is the point. God is in charge. People can choose to willingly work alongside Him, or they can be worked around.

Sovereignty, the fact that God is in charge, is a key theme in the book of Esther. He is in charge of all the things that have happened and are happening. He is moving in and through these events to accomplish His eternal purposes. In Esther's case, He is faithful in preserving the Jewish people, albeit from a place that seems unseen and with methods that make Him feel absent.

Okay. Here we go. Even if you have never read the book of Esther, you have most likely heard the phrase "for such a time as this." This Scripture, Esther 4:14, is one of the most quoted and recognized Scriptures today.

Mordecai is assuring Esther of the fact that God will provide another means of help. He is trusting God to keep His promise—the promise He made back in Genesis to Abraham, Isaac, and Jacob to sustain the Jewish people. Mordecai is leaning in and trying to impart the same trust to Esther.

Let's take a quick inventory of what Esther and Mordecai are up against. First, they are living in a kingdom that is outside of God's promised land. The king vacillates and is easily manipulated. The system of laws and government are malleable. And there seems to be an unchecked evil Haman in a powerful position of influence. The odds seem stacked. This, by all intents and purposes, looks to be an impossible task.

WRITE ESTHER 4:14 HERE.

I think it is interesting that Mordecai says "who knows" before his famous "for such a time as this" line. Who does know what the future holds? Not me. I don't know what tomorrow holds, but God certainly does.

Corrie ten Boom famously said, "Never be afraid to trust an unknown future to a known God." God, in His infinite wisdom, is not limited by time or space. He has unchangingly existed in yesterday, today, and in tomorrow. He is not surprised by what is coming.

Still, He summoned Esther to move. He summons us too.

FIND ACTS 17:22–27. WRITE VERSES 26 AND 27 HERE.

This passage is teaching us that God has planned our timing. He foreknew and chose the year we were born and the place we would live.

Why do you think God has placed you where you are? How is He summoning you to move—when and where you are now?

WEEK 4 | DAY 5

READ ESTHER CHAPTER 4.

SCRIPTURE FOCUS: Esther 4:15–17

Have you ever watched VH1's *Where Are They Now?* It was a docuseries in the early 2000s that showcased celebrities and what they had been up to after their fall from stardom. The show would flash back to the start of their careers and then fast-forward to their current ventures.

I often find that if we could flash back, our hindsight would most certainly be 20/20. We would see where we stepped rightly, or where we missed the mark, with clarity.

In this passage, we are witnessing the setup of what would be some of the greatest role reversals and plot twists in Jewish history.

Esther bravely decides to intervene, to go unsummoned before the king and plead for her people. She decides to trust the Lord and take the risk, grasping her own life in her hands to accomplish what God had summoned her for. Talk about "ride or die."

WHAT DOES SHE TELL MORDECAI TO DO IN VERSES 15–16?

When I became a new believer, I had never heard of fasting. This particular spiritual discipline was not something that was even on my radar in our culture of overconsumption and instant gratification.

What is a fast? A fast is simply a voluntary giving up of food for a while for spiritual purposes. Fasting reminds us of our fragility and of our utter dependence on God. After skipping a meal, my body begins to feel the effects. I'm slightly tired, even a little cranky. I want to satisfy my earthly need for food, but fasting reminds me that I hunger for God and need Him to sustain me.

When we fast, we say to God, "I am hungry for You and You alone." We proclaim with our actions that we love Him above all else. In our intentional act of fasting, we seek His will and direction for our lives.

Here are a few tips for fasting, if you are a beginner.

Don't overdo it. It is difficult to go from never fasting to fasting for days on end. Try skipping one meal one day a week. Gradually move to skipping two. Take it slow.

Plan what you will do instead of eating. Don't just go on a hunger strike. A friend of mine would get an empty plate, sit down at her table with her Bible, and turn her plate over—choosing to sit at the table and read her Bible instead. It was powerful.

Trust the Lord to lead you. Turning food down is not a means to manipulate God into moving, but instead is an act of submission to His will. Use this time to pray for wisdom, clarity, and courage to move.

Esther calls for a three-day fast, both during the day and the night. Prayer is not explicitly mentioned, but certainly implied. Psalm 35:13 links prayer and fasting. In the New Testament also, Paul in Acts 13:3 shares the practice of prayer and fasting.

Jesus Himself, in Matthew 6:16, says, "**When** you fast . . ." implying not *if* but *when* believers fast. Fasting is a spiritual discipline that draws us near to God, humbling ourselves in the process, so that we can honor and worship Him properly.

At the beginning of week four, we find Esther abdicating her responsibility to move, and now we find her responding to a great summoning—an act that has implications for an entire people. She can no longer continue living in the shadows. It is time to come out of hiding. Hiding her Jewish identity was possible no more. The time for courage and trust is now—"for such a time as this."

Esther was being invited to work alongside God at the risk of her own life.

What about us? Are we still "in hiding"? Do we look like "Persians," hiding our beliefs to fit in or fly under the radar? Is there something specific, a hard decision or frightening step, God is summoning you to?

Most likely, we will not be asked to take the risk of putting our lives on the line for God, but there is one thing that we know God is calling us all to risk for—the cause of Christ.

FIND MATTHEW 28:16–20 AND SUMMARIZE IT HERE.

What is Jesus commanding? He is saying that it is the job of *every* believer to make disciples, not only pastors or church ministry leaders or people on a committee. Each of us is being summoned to risk our reputations, our preferences, and our personal comfort for this mission: to share the gospel.

Why are we hesitant to move, even when Jesus promises to be with us? I think it's because we struggle with feeling like we won't measure up, that we aren't enough.

Here's the truth. Jesus is the only flawless and sinless person God has ever used to accomplish His purposes. Otherwise, He works with broken vessels. He uses regular, sin-soaked, and stubborn people. After all, that is all there is.

So let's ask ourselves two important questions. *Who are we?* and *Who do we belong to?*

Esther was fighting a losing identity battle. At the beginning of this week, she was clinging to the security of her title as Queen and identifying herself with the pagan culture in order to maintain her safety.

Through the urging of Mordecai, she has come to accept her identity as God's beloved daughter and is ready to boldly step forward in obedience. With reckless abandon, she lets go of all her excuses and submits herself to the will of the Lord. She willingly readies herself for whatever is coming.

We can learn from her that trusting God makes us bold. If we acknowledge that He is ultimately in control, and that He is faithful, we do not have to fear what lies on the horizon.

Just as Mordecai urged Esther, I want to impart to you that we have got to live with urgency. This world is passing away, and many will pass with it if we remain silent. We have got to pick up our identity as beloved children of Christ and conform ourselves to the Great Commission for God's glory.

I believe God is summoning us all to be brought in and sold out for the mission and purpose of Jesus. We have to take the risk. Let's risk it all, knowing that God is good and faithful.

We know that He is in fierce pursuit of His children. He wants them to know Him and to make Him known.

Take a moment to jot down a prayer, asking God to help you boldly proclaim His name and to remove your fear. Ask Him to stir your heart for the brokenhearted and the lost. Pray for perseverance to pursue God's children. Sister, take the risk. It is worth it.

SUMMONED

to Selflessness

WEEK 5 | DAY 1

READ ESTHER CHAPTER 5.

SCRIPTURE FOCUS: Esther 5:1–8

Shortly after my husband and I got married, a new TV show came out we loved to watch together. *Burn Notice* is a network program about a spy in Miami who had been "burned" and left for dead. The main character was always escaping dangerous situations with a toothpick, a Q-tip, or plastic explosives.

The show, more often than not, would end with a cliff-hanger. We would be on the edge of our seats, waiting with suspense to find out what happened next. (This was before direct streaming and it meant waiting a week between episodes.)

This is what is happening here. We left off with Esther proclaiming her commitment to intervene on behalf of her people, even to the cost of her own life. She ordered a three-day fast, with the participation of all her Jewish brothers and sisters, as well as her own handmaids.

After her three-night-and-day fast, she took off her fasting garb and put on her royal robes. Typically, fasting included wearing specific clothing to indicate humility and supplication such as Mordecai's wearing sackcloth. Her posture before God would have been one of self-denial and reflected her full dependence on Him.

If we were to read this text in its original Hebrew, it would have read, "Esther put on her royalty."

Let's set the scene. After the cliff-hanger we are left with in chapter 4, Esther—from rags to robes—slowly enters the inner court. The camera lenses widen to showcase her silhouette in the door of the throne room. The light begins to reflect off her royal and regal dress. The camera pans to the king, solemnly sitting on the throne. He catches a glimpse of her as she progresses toward him.

Do you see how the author is slowing the speed of the story down? The author is taking painstaking detail to describe the entryway and the king's position, and is intentionally building suspense.

Will Esther be killed on the spot? During this period of time, Persian kings would hold a golden scepter they would lower if they were willing to grant audience. Beside them would be a Persian soldier wielding a large axe who would be ready to execute the approaching person at the snap of a finger.[1] Esther's fears in approaching the king uninvited were certainly valid.

Both possibilities, life and death, are clearly in front of her as she takes each step.

WHAT HAPPENS TO ESTHER (ESTHER 5:2)?

The Hebrew word used here for "favor" is *chen* and it implies that he took compassion on her, that his heart had turned toward giving favor.[2]

WHAT DOES KING AHASUERUS SAY TO ESTHER?

This sounds quite generous, doesn't it! But he is not literally offering her half of all he owns. This phrase was common among Middle Eastern kings and simply means that he is willing to offer her a favor, a phrase that communicates goodwill and friendship.[3]

WHAT DOES ESTHER ASK HIM TO DO IN V. 4?

Were you surprised by her invitation? It seems like all of King Ahasuerus's banquets are lit. Something crazy is always happening at these things. So Esther baits him by inviting him to a smaller gathering, making sure to include Haman.

WHY DO YOU THINK SHE DOES THIS? DO YOU THINK SHE WASTED HER OPPORTUNITY?

I mean, she just went through all this trouble, threw on her ride or die T-shirt, and then passed on her opportunity to out Haman in the public court. Why?

This moment was the culmination of all the prayers and fasting of God's people. She had been shown mercy, and the king offered her his favor. But now Esther had to be clever.

She was about to make a pretty tough ask of the king. She would be asking that he revoke an irrevocable law, one that he had personally approved and sealed with his signet ring. Additionally, this request would cost the king the money he had taken from Haman, depleting his royal treasuries. Not to mention that Esther was running the risk that the king would suffer embarrassment for having to repeal his edict.

I don't know about you, but all this feels a little like an impossible task, a task that would require a miracle.

So instead of blurting out, "Haman is a bad dude and we need to right this awful wrong," she cunningly invites them both to a feast.

Even though the immediate threat of execution is gone, the destruction of the looming edict hangs over her head. Her moves must be calculated and she must rely greatly on the Lord's wisdom.

The king grants her request, fetches Haman, and joins her for a meal. Shortly after consuming copious amounts of wine, the king asks Esther again, "What is your wish?"

WHAT DOES ESTHER SAY IN V. 8?

Man. This girl is pushing it, isn't she? The author records Esther's pause in Esther 5:7. "My wish and my request is . . ." Something stopped her. Maybe it wasn't the right time, or possibly something else gave her pause. God was still working, and Esther, walking in step with His sovereign will, petitions for another party.

HAVE YOU EVER FELT THE URGE TO PAUSE, OR PLACE SOMETHING ON HOLD BECAUSE THE TIMING JUST FELT OFF?

I know I am sometimes guilty of kicking down doors that God has sovereignly closed. I don't always wait for His timing. Stubbornly, it is mostly because I have a timeline and schedule of my own. I bring my plans to God, presenting them to Him with a three-point action list and petitions for where I need Him to place His proverbial stamp of approval.

It seems Esther practically paused, waiting for God to move and make a way for her.

How can we learn from her and wait for the Lord?

IS THERE A PLACE WHERE YOU MIGHT BE "SHOVING IN" WHERE GOD IS CALLING YOU TO STAND STILL OR WAIT? CONFESS IT HERE AND ASK GOD TO REVEAL HIS WILL IN THE CIRCUMSTANCE.

WEEK 5 | DAY 2

READ ESTHER CHAPTER 5.

SCRIPTURE FOCUS: Esther 5:9–14

A few years ago, I was strolling through my favorite used bookstore and I found a treasure. Buried beneath a stack of old books was a first edition C. S. Lewis hardback of *The Screwtape Letters*. I audibly squealed as I picked it up. The inside page was signed by its previous owner. "Langdon Woods, November 1943" was gently penned in script.

This is the kind of book I will spend hours in, dog-earing pages and scribbling notes in the margins. C. S. Lewis is one of my absolute favorite authors. He has a way of saying things that sears God's Word into my heart.

In his book *Mere Christianity*, Lewis says, "The essential vice, the utmost evil, is Pride. Unchastity, anger, greed, drunkenness, and all that, are mere flea bites in comparison: it was through Pride that the devil became the devil: Pride leads to every other vice: it is the complete anti-God state of mind. . . . As long as you are proud you cannot know God at all. A proud man is always looking down on things and people; and of course, as long as you are looking down, you cannot see something that is above you."[4]

Pride is the sinister thing we are seeing in Haman now.

How quickly these warm and fuzzy feelings turn to ash and vengeful anger.
This sounds like an ego problem. Moments ago, Haman is feeling content as he is
wined and dined by the Persian royalty, but when a fellow court member refuses to
"tremble" before him, his pride and ego are wounded, sending him into a fit of rage.

Where have we seen this before? Oh yeah. King Ahasuerus, when Vashti refused
him and subsequently undermined his ego, also was consumed with anger. These
two make quite a pair.

FIND PROVERBS 16:18 AND COPY IT HERE.

NOW FIND JAMES 4:6. WHAT DOES IT SAY?

What does God say about pride? He says He heartily opposes it. He calls us to
humility. Not to the exaggerated and self-deprecating type of humility or false
modesty, but instead, He calls us to realize how great His holiness is compared to
our sinfulness. Proper humility is a grasped understanding that He is infinitely
holy and we are not—not even close.

WHAT ABOUT YOUR OWN PRIDE? IS THERE AN AREA WHERE PRIDE HAS SOWN SEEDS IN YOUR LIFE?

A close friend and mentor once asked me one of the most convicting questions I had ever heard. He said "Megan, if God wanted to humble you, where do you think He would focus His attention?"

Wow. Ouch. There are so many places where pride has a habit of sneaking in. When I read Esther 5:11–12, I can't help but count all the self-centered pronouns, and I am convicted.

We find Haman trapped in his prideful stance, restraining himself and venturing home for a venting session with his wife and friends. He is talking with *his* friends, *his* wife, *his* riches, *his* sons: *his, he, him.*

One of my favorite movies is *How to Lose a Guy in 10 Days.* There is a painfully awkward scene toward the end of the movie when the main character enters a stage and begins to sing, "You're So Vain" at her love interest. It's brutal, but that song is definitely on Haman's life soundtrack.

But is this song playing in the background of our lives as well? Do we really feel like everything really is all about us?

When we elevate ourselves to this level of importance—raising ourselves above God—it's called idolatry.

Haman made an idol out of his ego. Haman then turns to his wife and their friends to invite them to worship his idol with him.

No *How to Get Rid of Your Enemy in 10 Days.* Zeresh's solution was quicker. Done. Easy peasy. She takes the bait and begins to worship his ego right alongside him, urging him to remove the cause of his frustration with cold-blooded murder. That sounds like great advice . . . or not.

When a friend comes to us in search of wise counsel, do we offer life? Or do we unapologetically offer them the earthly wisdom of "kill it off"?

As a military spouse, I am aware that sometimes the military culture invites us into all kinds of calamity. Very seldom is the advice that's sought in public spaces or social media life-giving. We expect there to be a certain degree of crazy when we ask for public opinion, but what about when we are the wife or friend?

HOW CAN WE BE SURE WE ARE GIVING GODLY WISDOM?

Zeresh advises Haman to build gallows that fit his ego, about fifty cubits high (about eight stories tall). Most likely, this device would not be a modern hangman's rope and platform, but instead, a pointed pole to impale someone on. It was pretty gruesome.

The advice pleased Haman, so he had the gallows made. I imagine him to be feeling pretty impressed with himself. A plot has been made to eliminate his enemy. He had all his circumstances in hand and was eager to see his vengeful plan carried out. Ultimately, his plans for the destruction of others would be his own demise.

What we will find in the next few days are a series of substantial role reversals and plot twists. They may ring of coincidence, but if we begin to examine these events more closely, we will see the guiding hand of God Himself, moving and ordering things for His divine purposes.

As we close for today, let's reflect on our own hearts and strive to rid them of pride and malice. Take a moment to confess any pride your heart has harbored. Ask God to change your heart, to refresh you, and remind you of His grace and love.

WEEK 5 | DAY 3

READ ESTHER CHAPTER 6.

SCRIPTURE FOCUS: Esther 6:1–5

Yesterday, we left off with Esther seemingly dropping the ball and missing her opportunity to step in for God's people. She postpones her request, mid-sentence, and invites her husband and Haman to yet another feast.

Haman trots home, high on life. Abruptly, his mood shifts from satisfied to seething when he sees Mordecai at the king's gate. Mordecai, being unmoved by Haman's approach, sends Haman into a sulking rage. On his arrival home, Haman regurgitates his self-inflated perspective of himself to his wife and close friends. After following some poorly given advice, Haman constructs gallows, specifically an eight-story high impalement stick, for Mordecai to be thrust upon.

In the meantime, on the very same evening, King Ahasuerus is suffering from a little insomnia. Who knows why the king was losing sleep? Maybe the intrigue of Esther's request was looming overhead. Perhaps he was struggling with the anxieties of ruling. Either way, at this point in the story, the moon is up and so is the king.

WHAT DID THE KING ASK TO BE BROUGHT TO HIM?

While I was still taking college courses, I was studying the dynamics of congregational ministries (riveting stuff) and one of my assignments required that I read my local church's organizational rules and regulations. For me, it meant reading a copy of the "Book of Church Order" and writing a seven-page paper explaining its applications.

I think I may have some understanding as to why King Ahasuerus asked for the royal chronicles. Maybe he thought it would have the same effect as reading "The Book of Church Order" at 11:00 o'clock at night. It was sure to put him to sleep.

A familiar saying fits this situation. "God is never early and He is never late. He is right on time."

WHY DO YOU THINK KING AHASUERUS COULDN'T SLEEP? AND WHO DO YOU THINK CAUSED IT?

That's right. This is a God thing. God is steadily moving, working behind the scenes for His glory and the good of His people.

It is interesting to see that while Esther and Mordecai are soundly asleep, God was certainly not.

FIND PSALM 121:4 AND COPY IT HERE.

WHAT DOES THIS TEACH US ABOUT GOD?

Mordecai is now in imminent danger. Haman has already constructed the murder weapon. Esther could not have known his plan to murder her cousin. Mordecai also is none the wiser that his life is in extreme danger. Esther and Mordecai are most certainly not in control of the scenario. There is nothing to be done.

But . . . is that true? God, in His sovereignty (His control over all things), intervened on behalf of Mordecai and robbed the king of his beloved slumber.

In addition, there were any number of bad choices that our not-so-favorite king could have sought to put him to sleep. There were court jesters, bards or singers, concubines, or an open all-night bar. Instead, he calls for the annual reports. Another coincidence? I think not.

WHAT DID HE DISCOVER AS HIS SERVANT READ FROM THE CHRONICLES (SEE VV. 2–3)?

The king, now fully alert and no longer trying to doze off, is now stunned at his enormous and embarrassing mistake. Mordecai had foiled an assassination plan and nothing was done to recognize his efforts. This is just another indicator that the king is irresponsible and foolhardy. You see, rewarding loyalty was a way to guarantee a king's safety in those times. If you served the king well, you would be handsomely rewarded.

But Mordecai was not only passed over for reward, five years had flown by before the king was made aware of his error. Let's double-click on this timing. This is God's way of actively working in and through the circumstance and bringing His purposes to fruition.

WHAT DOES THE KING ASK NEXT?

King Ahasuerus doesn't have a video surveillance, but it's fun to think about if he had. When the king asks, "Who is in the court?" he isn't asking because he heard someone come in or he was made aware that someone was seeking an audience. Rather, par for the course, he needs an advisor to tell him what to do about his new problem. He needs someone to fix his mess. He made a mistake by failing to acknowledge Mordecai and now he wants to "phone a friend."

WHO JUST HAPPENED TO BE APPROACHING THE COURT AT THE MOMENT THE KING WAS LOOKING FOR ADVICE?

Yep. You've got it. Haman is dashing in the door at just the precise moment. What timing!

FIND PROVERBS 16:9 AND WRITE IT HERE.

FIND EPHESIANS 1:11. HOW WOULD YOU SUMMARIZE THIS VERSE?

FIND ROMANS 8:28 AND COPY IT HERE.

Think about the times in your life that God has made divine appointments and how He had worked in the background to bring things about. What happened? Can you see God's sovereign hand guiding and moving through the seasons of your life?

Take a moment to reflect on them here. Praise God for His timing, His providence, and how He moved on your behalf.

WEEK 5 | DAY 4

READ ESTHER CHAPTER 6.

SCRIPTURE FOCUS: Esther 6:6–9

I love British humor. What we are about to explore is nothing short of hilariously ironic slapstick humor. Cue Patsy, Monty Python's buddy with the coconut shells. The author of Esther intends it that way. As we read the next segment of Scripture on our journey through the book of Esther, you might have to laugh at the rapid and ridiculous turn of events for our boy Haman. His obscene pride is laughable and should pose as a warning to all of us when we place ourselves at the top of our priority list.

WHAT DOES THE KING ASK HAMAN IN V. 6?

Indeed. Haman is stumped for a second. Then he figured it out. *Whom would the king delight to honor more than me?* he asked himself. Wow. Rude.

Haman is so caught up in himself that he can't even think of anyone else who should be honored in his stead. Haman, being the king's number two man, is having trouble wrestling with his ego.

WHAT DOES HAMAN REPLY (SEE VV. 7–9)?

One of my favorite historical figures is Queen Victoria. A docuseries about her life that I enjoyed depicted her royal wardrobe, her castle, and other trappings of her reign. When I read this text, I thought, *This looks and sounds like a coronation.*

WHY DO YOU THINK HAMAN ASKS FOR THESE THINGS?

Haman is trying to declare himself equal to the king, and even possibly is setting himself up to steal the throne. If something were to happen to the king, who do you think could slip in easily, especially after the king himself had Haman paraded down the street in his own royal garb and on his royal mount?

Man. This guy is slick. It is almost unreal how much pride oozes out of him. Yuck.

While the primary message of the book of Esther is centered around God's sovereignty, the recurring issue of pride seems to be ever present. And it seems to show itself as a warning of what happens to those consumed by it.

As God's people, we should rid ourselves of the sin of pride. I don't know about you, but I don't want to follow Haman on the downward path of destruction.

How do we recognize pride? Well, for starters, we need to ask ourselves where we compare our strengths to someone else's weaknesses. Are we consciously taking an inventory of other people's lives and muttering, *At least I don't have that problem* under our breath?

If so, we should drop what we are doing right this instant and beg God to deliver us from being prideful.

Twentieth-century Scottish minister William Barclay has been widely quoted as saying, "Pride is the ground in which all other sins grow, and the parent from which all other sins come."

That is terrifying.

WHAT HAS THE SIN OF PRIDE GIVEN BIRTH TO IN YOUR LIFE?

WHAT WERE SOME OF THE CONSEQUENCES OF YOUR PRIDE?

I used to believe that God only wanted our perfection and our performances. I thought I was only as loved as I was able to earn love. I would say, "Look, God. Look at all I've done right today. I've cleaned my house, spoken softly to my children, read Your Bible for a few minutes, and now I'm off to my small group." I harbored pride when I felt like I was doing all things well.

I was puffed up when I was able to manage all of the tasks set before me, especially when I excelled at them. Maybe if I was domestic enough, or charitable enough. Perhaps if I was kind enough, or industrious. Maybe then, God could love me.

But this is not the message of the gospel. The message of the gospel frees us from living by a checklist or feeling like we are constantly in a hamster wheel, performing and earning the love of God. The cross frees us from the need to chase a life that harbors pride in our hearts.

On the cross, Christ has freely given us our reconciliation to God. In other words, God is no longer separated from us because of our sin. All our sins are forgiven in Jesus. They are no longer counted against us, and we can live in obedience out of our love for Him.

One of my favorite early American theologians says it perfectly. Jonathan Edwards has been cited as saying, "You contribute nothing to your salvation other than the sin that made it necessary."

We bring nothing to God that can save us. All we bring is sin. This should take the pride winds out of our proverbial sails.

But how do we turn away from the sin of pride?

FIND PROVERBS 18:12 AND WRITE IT HERE.

Humility is the antithesis to pride and is the proper approach to eradicating pride.

HOW WOULD YOU DEFINE HUMILITY?

To me, humility is having a proper view of God and of myself. God is so holy. He is pure righteousness, love, justice, and mercy. I am none of those things. Without His help, I can do nothing.

He, in His grace, has revealed to us in His Word who He is and what He wants. I can admit that I don't know all the answers and continually reorient my heart to hear His instruction.

Humility is realizing that I am utterly dependent on Him and have no hope of being self-sufficient. When we view ourselves properly through these terms, we can't help but humble ourselves before Him.

Haman is obviously lacking in the humility department. We will see just how this will play out in the coming verses. In the meantime, we have to reflect on the status of our own hearts. Take a moment to pray and ask God to reveal where pride has flourished, and ask for Him to help you become humble before Him.

WEEK 5 | DAY 5

READ ESTHER CHAPTER 6.

SCRIPTURE FOCUS: Esther 6:10–14

In 2015, one of the most dramatic role reversals happened on live television. Steve Harvey was hosting the 2015 Miss Universe Pageant and he was about to announce the winner. Two contestants were left, Miss Philippines and Miss Colombia.

He reads the results, announcing Miss Colombia as the 2015 Miss Universe. She is crowned, happy tears are flowing, and nearly four minutes goes by until the mistake is discovered. Miss Colombia was actually the first runner-up, not the winner. The tension in the room was palpable as Mr. Harvey proclaimed, "I have to apologize."

Miss Colombia stooped down so that the crown could be taken off of her head and given to another. By all accounts, Miss Colombia was gracious in having to relinquish the honor she'd held for just a few minutes. I'm pretty sure that Haman's reaction to the turn of events he was about to experience was quite different.

After giving the king a substantial laundry list of all the things he wanted that would showcase his own importance, he thought he had won. He would get a royal crown, royal clothing, and a royal steed. The public would know that he was a man of importance.

WHO DOES THE KING IDENTIFY AS THE MAN HE "DELIGHTS TO HONOR" (V. 10)?
WHAT WAS THE DISTINCTION KING AHASUERUS USED?

Imagine Haman's dismay at the announcement that all the things he had wished for himself would be given to his enemy—Mordecai *the Jew*.

I find it is interesting that the king could identify Mordecai as a Jew. It would seem, that in the king's gifting of this immense honor and show of appreciation, that Jews were not the enemies of the crown after all—contradicting Haman's accusations.

WHAT DO YOU THINK MORDECAI WAS FEELING OR THINKING AS HAMAN
APPROACHED HIM WITH THE KING'S GIFT?

Here comes Mordecai's sworn enemy. Haman invites him to be dressed in royal robes and with a royal crown. Then Haman proceeds to tell Mordecai that he will be led around on the royal steed while Haman himself shouts, "Thus shall it be done to the man whom the king delights to honor."

Are you familiar with the Publisher's Clearing House Sweepstakes? The TV commercials feature someone showing up at your door with an oversized check for a ton of money. I don't know if that is how Mordecai felt, but I am sure he might have been slightly overwhelmed.

Maybe this was God's way of giving Mordecai some encouragement, or even giving him an indicator, that things were being worked out for the Jewish people. I mean, this whole drama started off because of bad beef between these two dudes.

Maybe this "happenstance" of Mordecai being so publicly rewarded by the hands of his enemy also encouraged the Jewish people.

Another important principle to note is that we are not promised these rewards, but when they do come, they are sweet.

WHAT ARE SOME AREAS IN YOUR LIFE WHERE YOU ARE WORKING THAT YOU FEEL LIKE YOU NEED ACKNOWLEDGMENT?

WHAT HAPPENS WHEN THE WORK WE DO, OR THE TASKS WE COMPLETE, FEEL THANKLESS? DO WE LOOK AT THE MONOTONY OF SOME OF OUR RESPONSIBILITIES AND FEEL FRUSTRATED THAT WE AREN'T BEING RECOGNIZED?

I remember when my oldest daughter was two, and we had just brought our newborn son home. Every waking moment felt like a race to bedtime. By 8:00 p.m., I had changed the umpteenth diaper, washed the millionth sippy cup, and mopped up the billionth milk spill. My husband was working as an Air Force recruiter, pulling twelve-hour shifts, six days a week.

Needless to say, everything felt like a thankless endeavor. A couple of years later, when my husband deployed, the feeling only escalated. Not only was no one saying "thank you, you're a rock star," but the workload intensified. At the time, our children were five, three, and one. Being married but feeling single was overwhelming.

One day, I had coffee with a very sweet woman from our local church. She had stopped by my house unannounced with a hot and fresh cup from Starbucks. She stepped into my mess of a world and gave me a piece of advice I sorely needed.

Without shaming me for the mounds of dishes in my sink and the battlefield of broken toys on my floor (not to mention the laundry monster on my couch), she told me, "Consider everything you do a small act of worship."

"No one will say 'thank you' right now," she said. "Change your mind about why you do what you do. If you do all these daily things to worship God, and God alone, you won't need a 'thank you.'"

It seems that Haman's primary motivation for doing anything was to bring glory to himself. We are seeing now just how that mindset turns out. It isn't going well.

AFTER MORDECAI RETURNS TO THE KING'S GATE, WHAT DOES HAMAN DO?

Haman goes home in despair and riddled with shame. He skulks into his house and begins to complain to his wife and close friends. Haman is home just long enough to hear a pretty profound statement from them.

WHAT DO ZERESH AND HAMAN'S FRIENDS SAY TO HIM?

Wow. What a warning! All of a sudden, these friends of his, along with his wife, become master theologians.

FIND GENESIS 12:1–3 AND SUMMARIZE THOSE VERSES HERE.

When God makes a promise, He keeps it. Mordecai, along with all the Jews, were the family of Abraham. God preserves His people. Possibly Zeresh, Haman's wife, knew of this promise. She herself was not a Jew, so she could have just been terribly superstitious and viewed the day's events as an omen of what was to come for Haman. Who knows? But one thing is certain—Haman is going down.

In the middle of hearing about his impending doom, Haman is swept off by the king's eunuchs to Esther's feast. There's something I want to leave us with as we close today's reading.

Landon Dowden posed a question that rings in my mind when I think about today's Scripture. Dowden says, "There is no one that the Father wants to honor more than the Son. Why should we be just as eager to offer honor to Christ rather than seek it for ourselves?"[5]

SUMMONED
to Study

WEEK 6 | DAY 1

READ ESTHER CHAPTER 7.

SCRIPTURE FOCUS: Esther 7:1–4

Take two. Let's try the scene again.

This is the second of Esther's feasts. After the first banquet hosted by Esther, the king suffered from some slight insomnia and discovered that, through some seriously boring readings of the annual reports, Mordecai had prevented an assassination—a deed that had not been acknowledged or rewarded. The king rectified his mistake and commanded Haman to honor Mordecai publicly, parading him down the street on a royal steed with a new crown.

Haman, ashamed and embarrassed, heads back to his house to complain. With just enough time for his wife to warn him of his impending doom, he is whisked away to today's "wine and dine" with the king and queen.

I'm sure King Ahasuerus was sitting on pins and needles, waiting to hear what Queen Esther wanted. He asks again, with the catchphrase "Even to the half of my kingdom, it shall be fulfilled"—encouraging her that the king plans on being generous.

WHAT DOES ESTHER ASK THE KING FOR?

WHY DO YOU THINK SHE ASKS IN A POLITE AND SUBSERVIENT MANNER?

Esther is aware that the king is arrogant, foolhardy, and swiftly makes harsh decisions when defensive. So, cleverly, she begins with a phrase we see repeated over and over in the book of Esther. She says, "If I have found favor" and "If it please the king."

Pleasing the king seems to be the theme of this book, doesn't it? What will please the king? A queen in her royal diadem, shaking it for the crowd? No? What about a new harem full of women? A new queen? Money?

Being keenly in touch with the finicky nature of the king, Esther proceeds with caution. She asks for her life and for the lives of her people. She bravely and courageously reveals her identification as a Jew—right in front of Haman.

WHY DO YOU THINK SHE WAITED UNTIL THE SECOND DAY, WHEN SHE COULD HAVE DONE THIS THE DAY BEFORE?

I believe Esther was waiting for the Lord. In between these two shindigs, the Lord elevated Mordecai by orchestrating the king's sleeplessness and his subsequent discovery of Mordecai's lifesaving efforts.

HOW DO YOU THINK THE JEWISH PEOPLE FELT TO SEE MORDECAI WALKED THROUGH THE STREETS, LED BY HAMAN, BACK IN CHAPTER 6 VERSE 11?

Surely Esther was emboldened by this reversal from the Lord. I imagine her to be brimming with hope, as she has now witnessed that the Lord was moving and intervening for His people. But what about us? Do we wait for the Lord to move?

Sometimes I feel like I am the most impatient person on the planet. It's like I'm sitting on a hair trigger, ready to go off at 150 miles per hour at any given moment. I make my plans and I execute them—rather than waiting or resting to hear the Lord.

IS THERE SOMETHING YOU SHOULD BE PLACING BEFORE THE LORD, WAITING FOR HIM TO MOVE ON YOUR BEHALF?

Obviously, we can see what happens when plans are made without the Lord, and without His purposes in mind. Haman stands as a warning for those who would be prideful and consult their own worldly wisdom instead of the whole counsel of God. Haman, who was described as "the enemy of the Jews" was doomed from the beginning.

We can be sure that God is faithful and He keeps His promises.

But what has God promised us?

There is a seriously terrible proclamation rippling through the American church. The idea is that Christians are promised health, wealth, and prosperity. Many refer to this as the "prosperity gospel." This notion—that believers will never be poor, sick, or in suffering—is complete false.

We deal with discouragement, dreadful diagnoses, derelict bank accounts, and death. These things are simply part of the human experience this side of heaven. Is God with us through those things? Absolutely. He is with us when we are sick. He provides for us in our need. He comforts us in our suffering. But He doesn't always prevent them or interrupt our pain.

He never promised to.

What He did promise us is that He would raise us up on "the last day" in and through Jesus (John 6:40).

Our God is faithful; He never leaves or forsakes; His love is shown in His promises, namely in His son Jesus' sacrificial death, burial, and resurrection, and *not* in His provision of a continually comfortable or pleasing life.

Are you suffering long, friend? Take heart. Jesus, during His life here on earth, taught us that there will most certainly be trials and trouble in this world (John 16:33).

God has promised to be with us in our troubles, to provide a way for us to be reconciled to Him (made righteous), and to create access to Himself through Jesus. He's done it. It is finished.

In response, we can bravely face each new day. We can live expectantly that God is for us, moving and working (albeit that He sometimes feels unseen or inactive by our limited knowledge) for His glory and our good.

In Esther's case, her trust in the Lord manifested as courage. She, through the power of God, mustered her gumption and chose to reveal herself as a Jew—to share the fate of those condemned to death to save her people.

This scene showcases the tension between God's will and a person's responsibility to act. We have seen that God can, and will, work around people and accomplish His will Himself. However, we continually see that He chooses to work *with* people, not around them.

As we wrap up today, ask yourself if there is something God is trying to do *with* you, not *in spite* of you. Take a moment to reflect, jot down some praise, or pray.

WEEK 6 | DAY 2

READ ESTHER CHAPTER 7.

SCRIPTURE FOCUS: Esther 7:5–10

Well, she's gone and done it now. Esther has lit the flame on the Roman candle that is about to shoot off right in Haman's face.

When I was a kid, my favorite book was *Grover's Bad, Awful Day*. My mom would curl up with me and read it to me just about every day. My dad was deployed a lot when I was young, and the book helped me process some of my feelings through circumstances I couldn't control.

Poor Grover endured a never-ending stream of "bad day" events. His shoe got stuck in gum, his ice cream fell to the floor, and his picture was a flop. Nothing seemed to work for him on his "bad, awful day." Well, our boy Haman is about to have a pretty rough run through.

Esther had just laid out the problem before the king. She said, "For we have been sold, I and my people, to be destroyed, to be killed, and to be annihilated. If we had been sold merely as slaves, men and women, I would have been silent, for our affliction is not to be compared with the loss to the king" (Esther 7:4).

She was successful in rousing the king's interest, and even alluding to his own complicity. You see, without realizing it, he had signed Esther's death warrant as a Jewish woman. Not knowing that she was Jewish, and the fact that he allowed Haman free rein to do as he pleased, has created a problem.

Now he has to figure out a way to fix things, and Esther has perfectly primed him for a sympathetic response.

WHAT DID THE KING ASK IN VERSE 5?

WHAT WAS ESTHER'S RESPONSE?

WHAT DO YOU THINK HAMAN WAS FEELING?

WHAT WAS THE KING'S RESPONSE?

The king was so overcome with anger that he left the room. Haman, in his terror, fell down before the queen and begged for his life.

Isn't it ironic that the beginning of this book started out with Haman—a guy who was consumed with pride and raging over a Jewish man's refusal to bow to him— falls flat on his face and grovels before a Jewish woman? Cue Alanis again . . .

When the king returned to the room, he found Haman prostrate before Esther, falling down and begging. In Persia, it was a big taboo to come that close to the queen, or any woman in the king's court. The king misunderstood Haman's intent, thinking his pleading was an impending assault.

In response, Haman's face is covered and he is taken away. A eunuch, Harbona, announces that Haman had gallows built at his home and was plotting to kill Mordecai.

WHAT HAPPENS NEXT?

Yup. You got it. Haman is now being hanged (specifically, he is being impaled) on the post he had built for Mordecai. Yikes.

SINCE THESE GALLOWS WERE BUILT "FIFTY CUBITS HIGH," AND SINCE THE WHOLE CITY COULD MOST LIKELY SEE HAMAN'S DOOM, WHAT DO YOU SUPPOSE THE PEOPLE IN SUSA WERE THINKING?

We have a term in the South that we use when something like this happens: comeuppance. Haman got his comeuppance. It basically means he got what was coming to him. John MacArthur said it well. "Pride cost man Eden, and the fallen angels heaven. It doomed Sodom and Gomorrah. It cost Nebuchadnezzar his reason, Rehoboam his kingdom, Uzziah his health, and Haman his life."[1]

I think that, in Haman's case, dangling high above the city skyline sent a message: the God of Israel is the one true God. When Haman started messing around with God's chosen, he inadvertently threw the gauntlet down at the feet of the God of the universe. And God is not one anyone should want to "throw down" with.

Haman's death confirms, over and again, that God is sovereign and totally in control. Less than a day ago, this guy was living his best life, plotting revenge on Mordecai, and bragging about all his accomplishments and wealth. On a dime, pardon the pun, it seems that Haman's fortunes were turned.

The text ends with "Then the wrath of the king abated."

I can't help but camp out here for a second. We hear a lot about love in Christian spaces. We hear things like "God is love" and about how we are "loved." Those things are absolutely true. God *is* love (1 John 4:8). Love is one of His many attributes. In Christ Jesus, we are loved.

But do we even think about wrath? Wrath is strong or vengeful anger. God feels wrath toward our sin and, without Jesus, His wrath would stand against us. Because Christ has intervened for us and taken the punishment for our sins, we will not be subject to God's wrath.

In fact, God poured all His wrath out on Jesus at the cross. Iain Duguid says it this way: "Our King's wrath was poured out in full upon His own Son on the cross. And if God's fury has been poured out in full upon Christ, now there is none left for us (see Gal 3:13)."[2]

Hallelujah. Amen.

Because of Christ's finished work on the cross, my sins and your sins are no longer counted. The sin debt we owed to God has now been paid in full. We will no longer stand guilty, or spend eternity separated from the God who made us.

Let's spend some time contemplating Christ's great love for us in Romans 8:35–39 as we close today.

> Who shall separate us from the love of Christ? Shall tribulation, or distress, or persecution, or famine, or nakedness, or danger, or sword? As it is written,
>
> "For your sake we are being killed all the day long;
> we are regarded as sheep to be slaughtered."
>
> No, in all these things we are more than conquerors through him who loved us. For I am sure that neither death nor life, nor angels nor rulers, nor things present nor things to come, nor powers, nor height nor depth, nor anything else in all creation, will be able to separate us from the love of God in Christ Jesus our Lord.

WEEK 6 | DAY 3

READ ESTHER CHAPTER 8.

SCRIPTURE FOCUS: Esther 8:1–8

One of my favorite childhood movies was *The Wizard of Oz*. I was around eight or nine years old when I first saw the film. I had stayed home from school sick, and my mom had grabbed it as a rental from Blockbuster.

I watched the black and white scenes unfold before my eyes as Dorothy's house plopped down on top of the wicked witch. As the story goes on, Dorothy ventures out of her house and finds herself in a world of technicolor. An ethereal voice is singing while birds tweet in the background. The Munchkins begin to quietly move from their hiding places when it is announced that "the wicked witch is dead!" The whole crowd breaks out into song and a celebration ensues.

"Ding Dong," Haman is "not only merely dead, [he's] really most sincerely dead." The problem is that his edict is not. The decree proclaiming death and destruction for the Jews in Persia is still very much alive.

After Haman's death, the crown now owns all his possessions. In an attempt to make restitution toward Esther, the king gives her Haman's earthly wares. She now has control and possession of Haman's entire household—his home, his money, and so on.

The king gave Esther riches, specifically Haman's riches. Esther also shared with the king that Mordecai was in fact her cousin, which would make Mordecai and the king related by marriage. Then the king gave Mordecai Haman's position as the number two guy in Persia, literally handing him the royal signet ring.

Now Esther has great wealth and Mordecai has great power. But is that what they wanted? No. These gifts, while I am sure they appreciated them, did not make up for the fact that their people were still in grave danger.

What does Esther do then? She again intercedes for her people, pleading with the king to change the edict against the Jews in Persia.

The king's response sounds a little comical to me. In my head, it sounds like this. "Girl! I just gave you all this dude's stuff because he was acting foolish. I even made your cousin the second in command. What else do you want?"

More or less, Esther played to the king's emotional connection to her. Notice there is no mention of justice, right, or wrong. The only thing presented is, "If you loved me, you would . . ."

WHAT WAS SAID TO BE TRUE ABOUT PERSIAN LAWS? (ESTHER 8:8)

The law was irrevocable. Because Haman's law could not legally be changed, Mordecai and Esther were given permission to release a counter edict to challenge the existing decree.

I can't seem to get over the fact that this king is so weak-minded and morally loose. He doesn't care about the people. He only cares about his image in the court. He is apathetic. Esther, on the other hand, is described as being moved to tears and pleading for the safety of her people.

Esther's pleading reminded me of a time where I found myself pleading before the Lord.

Earlier that year, tragedy had struck. A young military spouse had committed suicide and it sent shockwaves through our military community. She had been so young and full of life. The circumstances around her passing were hard and the whole ordeal brought me to my knees.

I was heartbroken because I understood that this young woman suffered from the same loneliness and isolation many of us as military spouses feel on a regular basis. In her darkest moment, there was no one to turn to. She left this world feeling like there was no hope, and there was no one to tell her otherwise.

I fell on my face before the Lord, begging and pleading for more workers—more gospel communicators and mission workers for my brothers and sisters in the active duty service community.

IS THERE A PEOPLE GROUP YOU ARE PLEADING FOR?

The apathy of the world surrounding her suicide was gut-wrenching. Did anyone care? The local news covered the event, but will anyone remember her name? I know with absolute certainty that I will.

In a recent year, the Pentagon received a report on military family suicides. It was discovered that 186 military dependents (spouses and children) committed suicide in 2017.[3] One hundred twenty-three of these deaths were military spouses, other people in the same position I'm in.

Just like Esther went before the king pleading for her people, I also find myself pleading before the King.

FIND MATTHEW 9:37–38 AND WRITE IT HERE.

Here, Jesus is speaking to His disciples and instructing them to ask God for more workers. The English Standard Version says to "pray earnestly" to the Lord of the harvest.

Would you join me in praying earnestly that the Lord would send more workers into His harvest? Let's pray for your community and mine, that God would do a mighty work and send us as proclaimers of the gospel, alongside many others.

Father God,

As You reign in heaven, we labor here on earth for Your glory. You are so holy. We pray for Your kingdom to grow in our local places and for Your will for our cities, communities, and states to be done in Jesus' name. Send laborers out to proclaim Jesus—Your message and messenger of hope. We ask that the people in our places would be plugged into the life of a local church and be shepherded toward You. We pray for lost people to become found children. We pray earnestly that You would raise up revival for Your glory and our good. Amen.

Jot down a special prayer for the people you are pleading for. Ask God to intervene and send more workers.

WEEK 6 | DAY 4

READ ESTHER CHAPTER 8.

SCRIPTURE FOCUS: Esther 8:9–12

It's been about two months since Haman's edict had been issued. Originally, Haman cast lots, or Pur, to determine the date of destruction for the Jews. His decree for the death of all the Jews residing in the Persian Empire would have been carried out right before their celebration of Passover in the spring.

Now, two months later, a long series of role reversals and plot twists have landed us to this point in the story. Mordecai and Esther have both chosen to reveal themselves as Jews to the king. Haman has been destroyed and, in his place, Mordecai now wields Haman's power and position.

The month of Sivan on the Jewish calendar is during the May to June time frame. There are still about eight months to come before Mordecai and Esther's new decree will take place.

DO YOU RECOGNIZE THE VERBIAGE USED IN TODAY'S PASSAGE? FLIP BACK A FEW WEEKS AND REVISIT ESTHER 3:12–15.

See any similarities? The passages are almost verbatim, except some key differences.

FIND ESTHER 8:11. WHAT IS THE DIFFERENCE IN THE NEW DECREE FROM THAT WE READ ABOUT IN ESTHER 3? REMEMBER, THE ORIGINAL EDICT COULD NOT BE CANCELED.

Let's take a closer look.

The decree Haman issued included the mass genocide of an entire people. They would have been utterly defenseless and wiped from the face of the earth because it was law.

The governing officials essentially sanctioned a mass murder and looting session, declaring open season on God's chosen people. God would not let this stand.

The new decree doesn't reverse the existing edict, but instead, it competes with it.

Before, the Jews were not allowed to assemble. In the new decree, they can. According to the first edict, the Jews were forbidden to resist and defend their own lives. Now they can. The Jews have been given full permission to destroy, kill, and annihilate those who were perfectly positioned to destroy, kill, and annihilate them.

I find it really interesting that King Ahasuerus is unable and unwilling to change his own laws. He holds to a standard. God holds to His standards too.

Let's compare kings. God is omnipresent (everywhere all at once), omnipotent (all-powerful), and omniscient (all-knowing). His decisions are made from this place. He is everywhere, knows everything, and is sovereign in His control.

On the other hand, King Ahasuerus is foolhardy, easily influenced, and self-motivated. His choices stem from a place that puffs him up or creates pride. All throughout the book, we can see that he only concerns himself with his own foolish vanity.

God concerns Himself only with His glory.

WHAT DO YOU THINK THIS MEANS ABOUT EARTHLY RULERS?

CAN THEY COMPARE WITH GOD, THE SOVEREIGN RULER?

In ancient Persia, the kings were considered gods. They were revered as deity. The Bible calls this idolatry. In that cultural time period, God was not the center of existence. Instead, the king of Persia was placed as the centric and sovereign ruler that would wield authority over them.

In the Jewish culture, before God's people were exiled and living as a dispersed people in Persia, God was the center of life. He was infused into every aspect of daily living—from what the people ate to what they wore to how and when and where they worshiped. In cycles, the people would stray from His ways and even allow worship of pagan gods into their nation. God would punish them, typically through their enemies, until they repented. This cycle went on for hundreds of years. Finally God allowed the nation of Israel to be ravaged and the people removed from the land God had promised them and taken to Babylon (which was later conquered by Persia).[4]

The daily lives of the Jews living in Persia did not center around God and His ways. Why? Well, first of all, there was no temple. The temple in Jerusalem had been razed to the ground, and God's people were dispersed from their holy city. Second, during this exile in Persia, the Jews had to acclimate to their pagan neighbors.

Now, let's talk about us. Do we trust in our earthly rulers, deifying them, and forgetting that God is ultimately in control? Or do we dismiss their authority, screaming and anguishing over our grievances?

Here's what I mean. Just like our Persian counterparts, our modern culture is not centered around God. His worship is not the center point in American culture. Simultaneously, we often put too much faith in flawed earthly leaders, don't we?

What is the biblical perspective on earthly leaders and our subsequent submission to human authority? How do we deal with governing authorities that we don't like or disagree with?

The Bible shows us throughout its pages that God is in control of all things—even the leadership of humans.

FIND ROMANS 13:1-7 AND REFLECT.

If God has ordained all leaders for their appointed times, and instructs us to submit to the governing authorities, is there a time when we should stand in opposition or even rebel?

Scripture teaches us that we obey the government and the law of the land until those things force us to deny Jesus or abandon His teaching, that is, act in direct disobedience to Him.

Even still, we bear the consequences of our actions in response to disobeying governing authorities. After all, in some parts of the world, people are imprisoned, beaten, or even martyred for doing so.

Our job, as believers, is not to fight the government, but instead to further the cause of Christ as long as we are able.

We fight our battles through humility, not pride.

Here's the truth. Jesus is over even the highest office-holders in the country, but this same Jesus calls us into a posture of submission, submission to Him and the leaders the Father has ordained to rule.

How do you feel about submission to earthly rulers? Are you encouraged that, ultimately, God is in control? Or is it a wrestling point? Take a moment to reflect and ask God for wisdom.

WEEK 6 | DAY 5

READ ESTHER CHAPTER 8.

SCRIPTURE FOCUS: Esther 8:13–17

There is a new edict at play now. Haman's edict for the annihilation of the Jews was set and matched. During the month of Adar, our February/March time frame, the Jewish people were destined for destruction. About two months after Haman's edict, Mordecai and Esther release a counter proclamation, allowing the Jews to defend themselves by taking up arms and eliminating any who would come against them.

Is your head spinning from all the role reversals in this story yet?

The book began with a queen who refused to come before the king when summoned. As a result, she was removed from her position and banished. Esther, on the other hand, came before the king unsummoned and was exalted. Mordecai, a Jew, refused to bow before Haman. In the end, Haman bowed before Mordecai and publicly honored him, and not long after was himself executed on the pole he had built for Haman's demise.

Haman's death triggers one of the greatest role reversals in the book of Esther: Haman, who was high and lifted up by Ahasuerus, is now dead. His power, which he used to manipulate the king and to issue a declaration of destruction against God's people, now belongs to Mordecai. The script is flipped.

Where Haman once stood in power, Mordecai now holds the signet ring, the approval of the king, and the ability to counteract the evil plan Haman devised.

Karen Jobes, a commentator on Esther, says that "Mordecai has just effected a legalized war between the Jews of the Persian empire and any people of any nationality who might set themselves against the Jews."[5]

The same swift horses that carried Haman's evil edict out are now carrying a new message.

WHERE WAS THE DECREE ISSUED FIRST?

WHEN MORDECAI WENT OUT BEFORE THE PEOPLE, WHAT WAS HE WEARING?

Blue and white were the colors of the Persian Empire. A golden crown and purple linen implied royal significance. What a triumph the Jews must have seen in his appearance. Not too long ago, Mordecai had been dressed in sackcloth, representing the Jews' impending misfortune and annihilation. His rise to power and his royal garb must have encouraged the Jews in Persia, indicating that God was on the move.

WHAT WAS THE RESPONSE FROM THE JEWISH COMMUNITY IN PERSIA?

In addition to God's encouragement in Mordecai's outfitting, there is much rejoicing and gladness when Mordecai goes out among the people. How does that compare with the events following Haman's decree in Esther 3? God has done it again.

BUT, UP UNTIL THIS POINT, HAS GOD BEEN MENTIONED AT ALL?

Have you noticed that there has not been any mention of God whatsoever in any of the verses we have been studying? What could this mean?

The Jews, at that time, were living away from the promised land. The temple had been burned to the ground and God's presence had left them. They had been exiled in a foreign land and living, as we've said, in what many scholars call *diaspora*— meaning the Jews were living as a people dispersed from their nation as the result of their own sin and disobedience.

God's name is left out of the book of Esther on purpose by its author in order to raise a question in the reader's mind. Will God act and intervene on behalf of His people, away from the temple, the promised land, and when they are not living for His glory? Will God be faithful?

WHAT DO YOU THINK ABOUT GOD'S "ABSENCE" FROM THE BOOK OF ESTHER?

God's name being absent from the text in no way makes Him absent from the scene. The events that occurred in Esther, the role reversals and plot twists, cannot be mere serendipity or happenstance. In fact, all the events, ironic swaps, and miraculous turns point to God's sovereignty, to His ultimate control over all things.

Essentially, the heartbeat of this book is that God is good when things are bad. He moves in and through our circumstances, our choices, and even our disobedience.

Isn't it encouraging that God can and does move in our lives? He moves when we listen. He moves when we don't. He is sovereignly working behind the scenes, albeit sometimes unseen or unfelt, for His glory and our good.

FIND VERSES 16–17 AND SUMMARIZE THEM HERE.

AS THE NEWS OF MORDECAI AND ESTHER'S DECREE REACHES THE PERSIAN EMPIRE, THERE IS GLADNESS AND FEASTING, BUT WHAT ELSE HAPPENS IN ESTHER 8:17?

WHAT DO YOU THINK IT MEANT WHEN THE AUTHOR WROTE THAT MANY "DECLARED THEMSELVES AS JEWS, FOR FEAR OF THE JEWS HAD FALLEN ON THEM"?

This is historically the only place in Old Testament Scripture where it denotes many people in a foreign land coming to faith in God. The numbers must have been immense.

It is important to know that "declaring themselves" as Jews was not simply a spoken word or change of outward appearance. In the Septuagint—the original Greek translation of the Old Testament—this verse is recorded as many "were circumcised."[6]

Whoa. That is commitment. These people of Persia were not simply slapping a poster up on their doors, declaring "We believe in God" in order to avoid the coming calamity, but instead, they faithfully joined themselves to a spiritual community centered around the God of all creation.

As we end today, I want to leave us with the thought of carrying good news.

Mordecai and Esther drafted an edict that meant the Jews were no longer a helpless target without defense. Their new decree declared that they could stand up, take up arms, and fight the evil coming against them. Are we also given good news by God to carry to people in our local places? What would happen if we, too, boldly proclaimed Jesus as King and Savior, allowing people to take the Word of God and stand against evil? I am certain that there would be much rejoicing. Take a moment to reflect and jot down a prayer, asking God for courage to take His gospel to the world.

SUMMONED

to Sift the Scriptures

WEEK 7 | DAY 1

READ ESTHER CHAPTER 9.

SCRIPTURE FOCUS: Esther 9:1–4

As we pick up in chapter 9, we are given a quick summary at the beginning. "On the very day" that the Jews were destined for destruction, "the reverse occurred." There is no suspense or cliff-hanger here. The author of Esther quickly ushers us to the result of the drama. The Jews are victorious.

But honestly, I anticipate that this week's events will be tough to stomach for some of us. We are entering into gruesome and bloody territory. Slaughter and gore lie ahead. But turning the book of Esther into the PG-13 version will only detract us from the meaning and ultimately, the truth of what God's Word is teaching us.

Let's be committed to sitting and soaking up the upcoming passages, expectant that God will show up in the mess. Let's press in and be ready to hear what God has to say about Himself through the passages of the book of Esther. Ready? Let's go.

WHAT IS HAPPENING IN ESTHER 9:2?

Here, we find the Jews gathering in their local places to mount a defense. Who are they mounting a defense against? Yep. The answer is "those who hated them." This is an important detail. The Jews are not gathering to recklessly kill people, but instead, are rising up to defend themselves from the people who are planning to exterminate them underneath the authority of Haman's edict. The Jews are not the aggressors.

Verse 2 begins with the fact that fear has gripped the Persian people and "no one could stand against [the Jews]." There is an unseen force that seems to be at work. Some of them may understand that it is God, while some would attribute it to luck. Either way, the public has begun to fear God's people.

What about Mordecai? What's going on with him these days?

Mordecai also has become famous and powerful. Many of the governing figures have decided to help the Jews, for fear of Mordecai has taken hold of them.

The oppressors have lost power, and the oppressed have taken up their stance in ruling. You bet these guys are afraid. I imagine that the "officials, the satraps, and the governors" are beginning to realize they picked the wrong team.

There is a surface level lesson that I have seen many church leaders set on, glorifying the person of Mordecai accompanied with an exhortation to follow in his likeness. I have heard sermons where pastors urge their congregations in messages like "Follow Jesus and He'll make your name great!" or "Look at Mordecai. He did the Lord's will and now he is rich and famous." Some men and women are falsely assuming that the call to serve God in Christian ministry involves writing bestselling books and speaking at sold-out venues.

Let's be perfectly clear. God never promised a rags-to-riches story to any of us. Nowhere in the Bible does it say being a Christian will guarantee us a pleasing or prosperous life. In fact, Jesus actually promises us trouble and trials. He does say we will encounter difficulty, resentment, and hate on account of His name.

We have to lay down the ideals that being culturally Christian instills within us. Christ was never after a large social media following or a pastorate in a megachurch building. But instead, He was all in and sold out for redeeming God's chosen people with the finished work of the cross.

Before we get into the next few days, we have to set the stage for how we will view the events in the text. First, we have to examine the concept of a war that is justified.

For our purposes in studying the Bible, we'll simply define a justifiable war as God's sanction to eliminate the enemies of God by the hand of God's chosen people as agents. There are several examples in the Old Testament where God commanded for an entire people to be eradicated for His holy purposes.

Before you tune out, stay with me. I know the next few sections may sound way harsh, but we have to wrestle with the text. We should not shy away from difficult Scriptures, but instead, we should grapple—grasping, reaching, and fighting to understand. Take a deep breath. Here we go.

FIND 1 SAMUEL 15:2–3 AND READ IT.

NOW FLIP TO EXODUS, CHAPTER 17.

LAST, CHECK OUT DEUTERONOMY 25:17–19.

King Saul, as we read in 1 Samuel, was charged with eliminating the Amalekites, all of them, for their charges against God's people. The short story is that Saul did not obey the Lord. He took for himself the best livestock and took the king of the Amalekites, King Agag, alive.

Do you see the connection yet? King Agag? Haman, the Agagite? The enemy of the Jews?

There is a distinct connection here. Saul's disobedience would set off a chain of events that would lead us here, right to ancient Persia.

I think we tend to look at people as inherently good. If God would just give them more time, or be more compassionate, then the people in opposition to Him would eventually love Him. Right? Everything would be perfect. They would discover Him, know Him, obey Him, and love whom He loves.

Nope. That's not how it works. These passages are evidence of that.

The second thing we need to understand is that there have been two themes working in tandem, from the beginning of time: God's justice and God's grace.

In the garden of Eden, Adam and Eve were told by God that if they ate from the tree of the knowledge of good and evil (Genesis 2:16–17), they would surely die. We read in Genesis 3 how they rebelled against God and as a result, sin entered the world. They shifted blame before ultimately being held accountable for their actions. Instead of instant death, they were clothed by God and expelled from the garden. No longer would they walk in the cool of the day with their King, but they would work and toil under the sun.

This is a picture of God's grace plus His perfect justice.

In the passages to come, we will see God's grace and justice fleshed out between God's chosen people and their enemies. We will see the fallibility of humans, the sin-soaked nature of the human heart, and the vengeance that lives within all of us.

Karen Jobes puts it nicely: "From the beginning of time God's war has been against sin and evil. It is easy to think wrongly of sin and evil as being abstractions apart from people. We seem to want God to destroy sin and evil, but leave people alone. However, sin and evil do not exist apart from beings who sin and do evil, whether angelic or human."[1]

Maybe because I am a military spouse, I am overly familiar with the idea and function of war. I have seen the cost of combat, and the ripples of war have washed over our family. I live with war every day. For me, war is an old friend I never wanted but have become accustomed to.

WHAT ABOUT YOU? DOES WAR UPSET YOU? MAKE YOU ANGRY? MAKE YOU FEEL AFRAID OR POWERLESS? HOW DO YOU FEEL ABOUT WAR?

As we move into the next few days, ask God to show you where the trip wires are for you. What will hang you up from seeing His goodness? Will there be obstacles in the next few days of study? Take a moment to pray, asking God to help you see Him in the Word and help you understand more about Him.

WEEK 7 | DAY 2

READ ESTHER CHAPTER 9.

SCRIPTURE FOCUS: Esther 9:5–15

I try to read this text through the eyes I had as a new believer. I wouldn't have known what to do with a passage like this. There were other places in Scripture just like this one, which included death and massacre, that would bring me pause. One question ran through my mind. *Who is this God who orders His people to kill?*

What I found was that God works in and through all sorts of people and places. He is committed to working out His purposes—no matter the cost. In this case, before we go any further, let's take a look at this passage from the 30,000-foot view.

It would be really hard to understand the context of this passage without the understanding of the concept of a justifiable war from the viewpoint of God's sovereignty. Otherwise, this passage just seems like a senseless slaughter and a devastating loss of life.

God was using war to exact His justice. Specifically, He was moving in and through these means for the preservation of His people. From the aerial view, God is giving the people who would stand against His chosen children the justice they deserve, and He is faithful in preserving the people group that He had ultimately chosen to bring the Messiah into the world. Here it is, folks—His justice and grace in tandem.

We also have to view the events that have transpired here through the context of the rest of the book. Remember that leading up to this passage, we learned that the Jews were planning to defend themselves against people who attacked them on the thirteenth day of the month of Adar.

WHOSE NAMES ARE LISTED AMONG THOSE KILLED IN SUSA THE CITADEL (VV. 9–10)?

HOW MANY MEN WERE KILLED ON THE 13TH OF ADAR IN SUSA (VV. 6, 12)?

Because of what we know from the previous passages, we know this must mean the ten sons of Haman attacked Jews within the city walls. Jews were not the aggressors, so they must have been set upon by Haman's sons.

WHAT HAPPENS NEXT?

I would have loved to be a fly on the wall for this conversation. I imagine these two standing around their kitchen island, casually discussing their day. "So, honey. It looks like you and your cousin have had a good day! Just inside the city walls, over five hundred men have been put to the sword."

When I read it, there is a tone coming from Ahasuerus. He is so foolish that he almost seems impressed by the death of his countrymen. "So, dear, what else can I do for you?" he asks.

Here's where things get a little weird.

WHAT DOES ESTHER ASK FOR?

Esther replies with, "Well, babe, if it's good with you, I would love to do this again. Let's give my guys another day to continue the killing. Oh, and by the way, could you impale Haman's ten sons?"

I can't make up my mind as to how I feel about our girl here.

I mean, in one direction, she could be faced with serious opposition in the city's capital and one day wasn't enough to sufficiently eradicate the threat in Susa. Simultaneously, maybe the sight of Haman's tens sons gruesomely displayed on the same gallows as their father would serve as a reminder not to mess with God's children.

On the other hand, Esther could sort of resemble Don Vito Corleone from *The Godfather*. Her response seems cold and vengeful. There is no clear way to land in either direction because the text does not explain her motives or her feelings. The one thing we can take away is that, regardless of her motives, God's people were being preserved and would not perish.

WHAT DO YOU THINK? IS ESTHER A FAITHFUL AND BRAVE SERVANT OF GOD, OR IS SHE A STONE-COLD KILLER?

"So the king commanded this to be done. A decree was issued in Susa, and the ten sons of Haman were hanged. The Jews who were in Susa gathered also on the fourteenth day of the month of Adar and they killed 300 men in Susa, but they laid no hands on the plunder."

By the end of today's passage, 800 men, not women and children, were killed in Susa. So another way of saying this is that 800 men attempted to murder the Jews and plunder their belongings. In response, the Jews organized and defeated their attackers.

To refer to our earlier question of, *Who is this God who orders His people to kill?*

It is clear in this text, and in many others, that God has enemies. There are people who stand on the wrong side of battle lines, directly opposite the Lord Himself. Those who would stand and follow Haman's edict to "destroy, kill, and annihilate" God's people are bringing His judgment down onto themselves.

It is beyond unfortunate. What's more is that you and I would once be counted among His enemies. Without the finished work of Jesus, we would be enemies of the crown—still stuck in our sin and in open rebellion against Him.

God demands justice, and simultaneously, in His grace, He has freely given Jesus as the propitiation, the penal substitute, for our own sin. This means that Jesus has taken the punishment of death we so deserved, and instead, we are given unmerited favor and access to God in Christ alone.

Let's end today with that thought to meditate on. We have been given unmerited favor in that, in Christ, we have been reconciled to God. We are no longer enemies, but He calls us friends. We are no longer at war on the losing side of sin. Take a moment to praise God, enjoying Him fully in Jesus.

WEEK 7 | DAY 3

READ ESTHER CHAPTER 9.

SCRIPTURE FOCUS: Esther 9:16–19

Yesterday, we watched as the Jews in the city of Susa began to throw off their burden of living in fear. They rose up and conquered their enemies, people groups who would have eliminated them.

Have you heard the saying "kill or be killed"? Well, that was pretty much the reigning sentiment across the Persian Empire. Remember, the empire was only slightly smaller than the entire United States (2.9 million square miles vs. 3.7 million square miles).

ACROSS THE 127 PROVINCES OF KING AHASUERUS, HOW MANY PEOPLE ARE RECORDED AS BEING KILLED?

HOW ARE THESE WHO WERE PUT TO DEATH DESCRIBED?

Seventy-five thousand people is an immensely high casualty count. The number is somewhat shocking. The text also denotes that those who were killed "hated" the Jews. Again, considering that the Jews were on the defense and not acting as the aggressors, this text is painted in favor of God's mercy.

Our God is an evangelistic God. In the last chapter, we were told that many people "declared themselves Jews." Those who wanted mercy, received mercy. There were those whom God embraced and welcomed into His family.

And here's the truth in this text. God protects His chosen children and He keeps His promises to them.

FIND GENESIS 12:1–3 AND READ IT THROUGH.

As we've seen before, God has promised to bless the nations through the line of Abram. Eventually, God would change Abram's name to Abraham and, through his line, would bring Jesus into the world to reconcile it to Himself.

God could not allow His people to be wiped from the face of the earth, because He cannot and will not break His promise to His people. He promised to preserve them, and preserve them He does.

For His people to be saved, they would have to take up arms and defend themselves. This would, without a doubt, be a scary endeavor. But nonetheless, God's people picked up arms and fought their enemy.

WHAT DOES ESTHER 9:16 SAY THEY DID NOT DO?

You might remember that the edict Mordecai and Esther had drafted allowed permission for the Jews to "gather to defend their lives, to destroy, to kill, and to annihilate any armed force of any people or province that might attack them, children and women included, and to plunder their goods" (Esther 8:11). But

Esther 9:16 says they did not take any plunder (*plunder* being goods and valuables from the enemy). Why not? They had express permission from the king.

WHY DO YOU THINK THE JEWS PASSED ON TAKING THE PLUNDER?

This phrase "but they laid no hands on the plunder" is repeated three times and signifies that it is an important detail. Because the original audience would have understood this as a war with the holy intent of saving God's people, they would not have wanted to financially benefit from their oppressors. They also did not want to repeat King Saul's folly in raiding and looting his enemies, lining his pockets with ill-gained profit.

WHAT DID THE JEWS DO ON THE 14TH DAY OF ADAR (ESTHER 9:17)?

Here lies another role reversal. First the Jews fast and now they feast. They rest and celebrate their victory by feasting. Outsiders became insiders as well, and they are feasting too. To them, the fourteenth day of Adar was a day to give back to one another by giving gifts of food.

A few years ago, my next-door neighbor's daughter wanted to celebrate her birthday by serving and giving back to her local community. The young girl decided to collect dog food, pet treats, and animal toys for the local pet shelter. On her birthday, her mom drove her up to the animal shelter with a minivan full of goodies that had been donated. It was beyond sweet.

I took a lesson from her generosity. Because she was able to celebrate another year of life, it inspired her to serve.

In our text today, the Persian Jews serve one another in response to God's grace and mercy.

When we experience the grace of God, it should lead us to serve each other in love.

Last year, a few of my fellow military spouses wanted to serve out of the abundance God had shown them. In response to God's love and grace, they challenged the military community to complete one million acts of kindness on Giving Tuesday. They urged the military community to think about ways that they could be kind to their local communities, perform an act of kindness, and snap a photo to share on social media with the #GivingTuesdayMilitary.

Over one million acts of kindness were given and the hashtag was trending on social media. I was overcome with emotion as I scrolled through each photo. So many people had been positively affected by the kindness and encouragement of another.

God's grace should urge us on to serve.

WHAT CAN YOU DO TO SERVE THOSE AROUND YOU?

IS THERE A TANGIBLE WAY YOU COULD GIVE TO YOUR LOCAL BODY OF BELIEVERS OR SERVE IN YOUR LOCAL CHURCH AS A RESULT OF GOD'S GRACE?

AS YOU PONDER HOW YOU COULD SERVE, TAKE A MOMENT TO PRAY. ASK GOD FOR CLARITY AND DISCERNMENT IN HOW YOU CAN GLORIFY HIM THROUGH SERVICE.

WEEK 7 | DAY 4

READ ESTHER CHAPTER 9.

SCRIPTURE FOCUS: Esther 9:20–28

Mordecai recorded the account of all that had happened and he wrote a second letter to the Persian Jews, urging them to keep these days for rest and feasting. The Jews accepted Mordecai's petitions and began to set the fourteenth and fifteenth of the month of Adar as a day for holy celebration.

I live on the Mississippi Gulf Coast and there always seems to be a reason to celebrate. Every weekend there is one festival or another. Everybody is looking for a good time and a reason to eat well.

We, as Americans, love to celebrate. We have so many days of holy observance as well as national holidays. Christmas is an entire experience at our house. I have nearly thirteen huge Rubbermaid tubs full of holiday decor. The same goes for the other major Christian holidays. Easter brings tons of pastel colors and messy egg dye. I love a good holiday celebration.

WHAT ABOUT YOU? WHAT ARE SOME OF THE BIG CELEBRATIONS AT YOUR HOUSE?

Today's reading is giving us a history of the implementation of the feast of Purim, a celebration that Mordecai urges all the Jews in Persia to observe. In the rural towns, the fourteenth and fifteenth days of Adar were to be set aside for celebration as a day of remembrance.

I wear a silver bracelet on my arm every day. It was a gift from a very dear friend, a KIA bracelet that is embossed with the name of her late husband on the front. Staff Sergeant Michael H. Simpson was killed in action on May 1, 2013.

He was on a mission in enemy territory when his ATV rolled over an IED, an improvised explosive device. He was thrown back into the blast crater. In the process of being medically evacuated, he leaned over to the man on his right and said, "Wife. Kids. I love." About ten minutes out of Ghazni, Mike went into cardiac arrest. He left a legacy of love in his wife, Krista, and their two sons. I know and treasure remembrance. I remember his sacrifice every day and I am committed to sharing his story. He shall be remembered and his sacrifice known.

Remembrance is what Mordecai is calling God's people to commit to in this passage.

WHY DO YOU THINK REMEMBRANCE IS IMPORTANT?

For centuries now, the scroll of Esther has been read in Jewish synagogues all over the world. When Haman's name is read, people stamp their feet or hiss. Children are given rattling noisemakers to shake while people shout "May he be accursed!" or "Blot his name from history!"

Pastries called "Haman's ears" are made, festivals take place, and there is rejoicing as people recount God's deliverance.

Can you imagine what the feasts of Purim looked like during the Nazi occupations?

The feast of Purim, or the Feast of Lots, is one of only two feasts not commanded in the Pentateuch—the first five books of the Old Testament, which that were written by Moses. This non-Mosaic feast is considered just as important as the feasts that the Jews were required to observe.[2] This section of the text is most likely included to explain how the Feast of Lots came to be part of the Jewish calendar.

Mordecai wanted the Jews to remember what God had done for them. They had been delivered from the hands of their enemies and preserved. God had kept His promise, and they were to celebrate to remind themselves constantly of His faithfulness.

What about us? Is there something we should be celebrating? We should celebrate every weekend. We celebrate our own deliverance—not from Haman and the Persian king's stupidity—but from the amazing salvation we are given in Jesus by attending worship. We honor what God has done through the preaching and teaching of God's Word.

The local church is one of God's greatest gifts to us, and to the world. The church has always been God's Plan A for reaching the lost. There is no Plan B.

We have heard that one does not have to be in church to be a Christian, but I would argue that a Christian who is outside of the shepherding of a local church is outside of the will of God. God desires for His people to come together in His name, for worship and learning.

Another amazing act of remembrance that is done within the local church is the remembrance of what Christ has done on the cross, the Lord's Supper, also called Communion.

So we also have a "feast" we participate in to keep the finished work of Jesus fresh in our hearts and minds. This feast was not given to us in a letter or by the recommendation of an earthly leader. This feast was given to us by Jesus Himself.

DOES YOUR CHURCH REGULARLY SHARE IN THE LORD'S SUPPER?

The institution of the Lord's Supper was meant to bring us communally together for the purpose of remembering that Christ's sacrificial death and miraculous resurrection have reconciled us back to God. All the wrath that our sins deserved has been placed on Jesus instead. We are then given His righteousness, and God views us as holy and blameless.

Isn't this something to celebrate!

As we wrap up today's passage, let's take a moment to reflect on all the days we celebrate as holy. Are our Christmas holidays, or Easter, just more commercialized and secularized days for consumption? Or are they sacred and set aside for holy use?

Take a moment to pray and ask God to show us where we have missed the real reason we celebrate. Ask Him to change our minds and hearts toward the significance of these days, bringing us back to a place where Christ is the centerpiece.

WEEK 7 | DAY 5

READ ESTHER CHAPTERS 9 AND 10.

SCRIPTURE FOCUS: Esther 9:29–32; 10:1–3

Two things are happening in the text here. I combined the last few verses of chapter 9 with chapter 10 because I want us to see something. Everything has changed, but nothing really has.

The first thing is that Esther sent out another letter, confirming Mordecai's account and authority. The phrase "peace and truth" in verse 30 seems to indicate that there may have been some disbelief or conflict between the Jews. It seemed necessary that "peace and truth" needed to be spoken in order to confirm what actually happened and how.

Esther confirms the practices of fasting and lamenting, obligating the Jewish people to continue the tradition year after year, so that they may remember all that had happened.

FIND ESTHER 10:1. WHAT HAS AHASUERUS DONE?

Does it seem strange that the first line in chapter 10 is about taxes? I mean, what does that have to do with anything? It seems this chapter is an epilogue of sorts— like a postscript to a really long letter.

While the imminent threat of Haman is gone, the same ruler is still in power and it is back to business as usual.

The king has been a problem through the entire book, showcasing his weakness of mind and constantly being directed by whoever was closest to him. The Jews have been delivered from their destruction, but they have not been defended from the damaging leadership of a weak-minded king.

Things will be good from here on out for the Jews, right? The threat of being wiped from the face of the earth is gone. Now aren't they free to live happily ever after?

I think this part of the passage gives us a cue that it won't be fine.

Here's the truth. God secured safety for the Jews—really their survival—but He had not yet secured their salvation.

God had preserved His people and kept His promise. He was working out His purposes, namely the purpose of bringing Christ into the world through the line of His chosen people, the Jews.

Nearly five hundred years later, a virgin would give birth to the Son of God, the Messiah.

As we come to the end of the last chapter in Esther, the author tells us that all the accounts regarding Mordecai have been documented and recorded in the royal Chronicles of the Medes and Persians. He was second in rank to the king.

The passage says he "was great among the Jews and popular with the multitude of his brothers, for he sought the welfare of his people and spoke peace to all his people" (10:3).

Mordecai was not a pastor or a preacher. Nor was he a prophet or king. He was a man in politics who lived a life surrendered to the Lord. God grew his influence and blessed his efforts.

We can learn a great deal from Mordecai, and from Esther, too, for that matter. We see from their stories that, once they identified themselves as God's children, they became bold and fierce in the efforts to serve Him. We can witness the blessings and interventions the Lord completed providentially on their behalf.

But we should be careful of modeling ourselves after any biblical character. After all, Jesus is who we are striving to be like. His characteristics are those we strive to acquire. Jesus Himself is a better mediator than Esther and a greater leader than Mordecai.

Esther and Mordecai did great things, and with the provision of the Lord, they aided in saving God's people with their obedience. But this story was never about either of them. At the center of the book of Esther is the person of God—moving quietly behind the scenes and proving His unending faithfulness to His people.

At the end of the day, God is the hero of the story of Esther. I pray that He would be the hero of our story as well.

SUMMONED

to Serve

WEEK 8 | OUR RESPONSE

Congratulations! You have just walked, verse by verse, through an entire book of the Bible. You have used sound Bible study methods and have learned to ask key questions of the text. Now you can go anywhere in the Bible and begin to grasp what God is saying. Today is our last session together. This will be a time of reflection and response.

My greatest hope and prayer for you is that the door to biblical wisdom and understanding has been unlocked. I pray that the hinges of hinderance would fly off the doorframe as it swings open wide enough for you to blaze through—with a powerful hunger to know the Lord and make Him known.

Start running your race, with the Word in hand, and never look back, friend.

Now that we have read the book of Esther, what should we do with all our newfound information? How should we adjust or calibrate our lives to match in response to the things we have found in the text?

Our focus throughout the book of Esther has been God's unchanging faithfulness. God is good when things are bad. He intervenes for us and invites us to labor alongside Him for our good and for His glory.

One thing that had the most impact on me during my time in Esther, aside from the awe and wonder of God's sovereignty, is that Esther's story is a parallel to Moses and the Exodus.

Did you catch it? Esther's bravery and obedience to the Lord in going unsummoned before the king is as profound as Moses standing before Pharaoh to set his people free. In both accounts, God faithfully delivered His people and worked in and through them to accomplish His purposes.

I wholeheartedly believe that if Esther had failed, God would not have. He is capable of working His purposes in and through the lives of His people. But in this case, Esther willingly played a part in God's saving plan for His people. With her, God delivered His people and made it possible for the temple to be rebuilt. Through God's provision, Esther led the charge for the reestablishment of God's people. Approximately twenty years later, Ezra would return to Jerusalem. Thirteen years after that, Nehemiah returned to Jerusalem.

Nehemiah, who led the effort to rebuild the city walls of Jerusalem, served King Ahasuerus's son (Artaxerxes) as a cupbearer. What do you think Esther's influence must have been at the Persian court?

Women have a calling on their lives from the Lord that is alive and well. God uses women and calls them to come alongside Him to serve. Throughout the centuries, women like Esther, Deborah, and Huldah have stepped into the Lord's service.

We know what Esther has done. Deborah and Huldah were prophetesses, declaring God's will for the nation of Israel. Deborah's story is told in Judges 4 and 5. Huldah is mentioned in 2 Kings 22:14. Hannah was the first to name God the "Lord of hosts" in her poignant prayer for a child in 1 Samuel 1:11. Lydia was instrumental in the church established in Philippi (Acts 16:11–15, 40). Priscilla taught Apollos, an apostle of Christ, who needed to understand the faith more fully (Acts 18:24–28). Chloe planted a place of worship in her home (1 Corinthians 1:10–11). Phoebe served Paul and carried the letter to the Roman church (Romans 16:1–2). Several other women are commended in Paul's personal greetings in Romans 16: Prisca again (Priscilla was a nickname for Prisca), Mary, Tryphena, Tryphosa, Persis, Junia, Rufus's mother, Nereus's sister, and Julia.

Women have worth. God calls us to bravely answer and live as a people all in and sold out for the mission and purpose of Jesus.

I have been camping out in Esther for nearly the last two years. While taking an Old Testament Theology course at Moody Bible Institute in Chicago, someone asked a question through the online discussion board that spurred this study forward (a question we touched on in week two). "Is Esther a harlot who lost her virginity to her Gentile husband, or is she a heroine?"

What a thing to ask, I thought. The longer I sat with the question, the more frustrated I became. First of all, Esther is not a harlot at all. She was a woman taken forcibly into captivity and turned into a sex slave, albeit a sex slave who became a queen.

She had very little, if any at all, control over her life. She was an orphaned child and most likely suffered a great deal of pain and anguish as she struggled to survive in a harsh and unrelenting environment. And she did exhibit great courage and valor in the face of danger.

I think someone should make this T-shirt: Ride or Die. Esther 4:16.

Then I thought, *Why can't she be both broken and bold?*

It occurred to me we tend to think in terms of black and white, or one or the other. She was indeed a broken and wounded woman, forced into a lifestyle that was lonely, painful, and full of fear. Simultaneously, in spite of all of it, she served God with reckless abandon.

If she can, we can too. You have something to offer the Lord.

WHAT DO YOU BELIEVE YOU HAVE TO OFFER GOD?

REFLECT ON WHAT 1 CORINTHIANS 1:26-30 SAYS TO YOU. IT IS WRITTEN FOR
YOU BELOW IN THE NEW INTERNATIONAL VERSION (NIV).

> Brothers and sisters, think of what you were when you were called. Not many
> of you were wise by human standards; not many were influential; not many
> were of noble birth. But God chose the foolish things of the world to shame
> the wise; God chose the weak things of the world to shame the strong. God
> chose the lowly things of this world and the despised things—and the things
> that are not—to nullify the things that are, so that no one may boast before
> him. It is because of him that you are in Christ Jesus, who has become for us
> wisdom from God—that is, our righteousness, holiness and redemption.

God can and does work through our pasts, our pain, and our passions. He uses
the things that have happened to us and will happen to us for His glory. There is
nothing He is not willing and able to use to bring Himself glory.

So view your story through new eyes, opening your mind to the possibility that all
things can be redeemed by God. No place or point in the narrative of your life is
wasted. All of it can be perfectly purposed for God's plan.

Another thing that is abundantly clear in the pages of Esther is the foreshadowing
of Christ.

Esther was being prepared as a mediator for God's people before she was actually
needed. She was made queen before Haman came to power and devised his evil
plan to eradicate God's people. In the garden of Eden, God was preparing His own
mediator.

This is one of my favorite passages of all time.

I have a rather large tattoo on my forearm depicting Mary, the mother of Jesus, and Eve; they are facing each other. Eve's face is downcast and covered in shame. Wrapped around her left leg is the tail of a green snake. She holds a piece of fruit in her right hand, with her other hand gently placed on the pregnant belly of Jesus' mother. Simultaneously, Mary is sweetly holding Eve's hand and lovingly touching her face with the other hand, as to give her encouragement. Mary is also firmly standing on the snake's head.[1] (Be sure to look up this endnote for information about this image.)

Jesus was always the plan. The theological term used to describe what is happening here in Genesis 3 is the *protoevangelium*—or "the first gospel." This is the first place where Jesus appears in Scripture—in the first book of the Bible, at the beginning of the fallenness of man.

In addition, Esther's fasting for three days before presenting herself before King Ahasuerus also points to Christ and His three-day period of physical death that was accomplished at the cross. According to *The Moody Bible Commentary*, the three-day period suggests that fasting was perceived as "self-affliction."[2] Esther's affliction, along with Jesus' affliction, ended on the third day.

In the same way, before Esther's appearance before the king, she left her rags and sackcloth to be clothed in royal garb. Jesus also was resurrected in glory before His King, our Father in heaven.

Ultimately, Esther's acceptance by the king meant the safety of her people and deliverance from the hands of evil. That Jesus' sacrifice was accepted by the Father meant salvation for all people, Jews and Gentiles, making us part of the family of God.

The most poignant allusion to Jesus in Esther is, in fact, the gallows made for Mordecai. On the pole meant to kill us all lies our greatest victory. Oh, what a foreshadowing of Christ's sacrifice.

He died the death we deserved in order to impart to us His righteousness. He paid the full penalty of all our sins and made Himself the substitution. God effectively poured out all His wrath onto Christ, so that we may be reconciled to Himself.

We have the gospel in hand. Its words are planted deep within our hearts. We have been given the greatest gift, in that Jesus died for us and in our place.

Now what do we do with it?

FIND MATTHEW 28:16–20. WHAT DOES JESUS SAY ABOUT HIMSELF? WHAT DOES HE INSTRUCT HIS DISCIPLES? ARE WE INCLUDED IN THIS INSTRUCTION? WHERE WILL THE POWER COME FROM TO CARRY THIS OUT (SEE ACTS 1:8)?

We have been charged by Jesus Himself to carry His redemptive story to the four corners of the world, making disciples (followers of Christ) through teaching and baptizing. In verse 19, the Scripture says "go." We may think this means we must travel far, or spend years abroad on mission to share Jesus with those across oceans, land, and sea.

Our mission field is in our own backyard. It lies in your family, your neighbors, your coworkers, your friends, and in your surroundings.

Essentially, as we "go" about our daily lives, we are supposed to love people so much that we can't help but share the greatest news there ever was with them.[3]

And here is the news.

FIND 1 CORINTHIANS 15:1–4 AND SUMMARIZE IT BELOW.

This is the gospel. This is the message we share.

Christ died for our sins. He died and was raised on the third day. With His resurrection, we have been made right with God and given free access to Him.

You might be asking, *That sounds great, Megan. But what does this look like in practicality? How do I live gospel-centered or on mission?*

The answer? It begins with your personal awareness and acceptance of the gospel. Have you actually surrendered your life to Jesus, or have you been on a journey in the painful pursuit of perfection?

The journey of the Christian life begins, is sustained, and ends with the gospel (summarized in 1 Corinthians 15:1–4). It is the beginning, the middle, and the finish. The gospel affects every aspect of daily life. It drives the way we love, the way we choose, and the behaviors we allow. It informs our beliefs and shapes our view of the world. The gospel is the hinge on which all else hangs.

Once we grapple with and work out our own salvation, we begin to desire the same freedom for those we love. We share the gospel with our spouses and children. We outreach in our neighborhoods. We plant within the confines of a local body, the church. We live the Christian life in community, not as lone rangers.

Ultimately, we fundamentally understand the missional nature of community.

FIND ACTS 2:42–47. WHAT ARE SOME WAYS IN WHICH MEMBERS OF THE EARLIEST CONGREGATIONS LIVED IN COMMUNITY?

The caption above this passage in my Bible says "The Fellowship of the Believers." The "apostles' teaching" is the Word of God. They valued being together. "Breaking of bread" is referring to corporate worship. They were taking the Lord's Supper and fervently praying for one another.

This is what the gospel-centered life looks like, a dedication to the authoritative Word of God, a healthy and flourishing prayer life, a commitment to a local church and loving fellowship. This drives the gospel and pushes it farther into our homes, our neighborhoods, our cities, and beyond.

Will we answer our own summons from the Lord to be ambassadors for Christ, or will we stay silent, apathetic, and unmoved for those still waiting for His deliverance?

Mission exists because God doesn't get the worship He deserves. We should long to see those who are wandering in darkness abounding in His light. There is an unmatched joy in surrendering our lives for the glory of the Lord and the expanse of His kingdom. Our Father is summoning us to walk alongside Him and to partake in the mission and purpose of Jesus—the Great Commission.

Matthew 28:16–20 says,

> Now the eleven disciples went to Galilee, to the mountain to which Jesus had directed them. And when they saw him they worshiped him, but some doubted. And Jesus came and said to them, "All authority in heaven and on earth has been given to me. Go therefore and make disciples of all nations, baptizing them in the name of the Father and of the Son and of the Holy Spirit, teaching them to observe all that I have commanded you. And behold, I am with you always, to the end of the age.

Jesus was not only speaking to those who were bought in and sold out for His mission. He also spoke to those who doubted. He commanded all His disciples—the devoted and the doubting—to "go" and make disciples. He encouraged them that He was with them.

Here is the beautiful truth. He is with us too. Let's accept our summons to share the hope we have in Christ Jesus with reckless abandon, serve with radical hospitality, and live freely with an overwhelming sense of loving kindness.

Our King is calling. Will we answer?

ACKNOWLEDGMENTS

To My Family: Keith, thank you for serving faithfully alongside me, for leading our family well, and ordering more pizza than any man should. You are the glue that holds this family together. You are a noble, supportive, and compassionate partner—deserving of all my respect. I love you beyond what words can express. To Hannah, Beau, Noah, and Carole, thank you for being patient and giving Mommy grace for all the office hours this book required. It is finally finished! May this book, and many more, be a recording of my deep reverence for God's Word, my insatiable love of the Lord, and my undying belief in Jesus as our Savior. May you learn to walk with the Lord in love. "Be imitators of me, as I am of Christ" (1 Corinthians 11:1).

To My Mom: Who would have thought, right? Thank you for putting up with all my craziness over the years. More than ever, I appreciate your wisdom and unwavering commitment to be there for me and my family. I love you and I hope I've made you proud.

To Our Family Pastors: Dr. Blake Henderson of Sola Church, your discipleship has been one of my utmost privileges. Thank you for investing your time into teaching me, correcting me, and encouraging me. I wouldn't be here without your support. Justin Daniel of Vaughn Forest Church, I'm beyond grateful for your steadfast instruction, guidance, and fellowship. Thanks for always picking up the phone—especially if it was to listen to entire chapters of this study. Paul Bankson of Houston Lake Presbyterian, thank you for giving our family a church home away from home. Your elders and congregation members are exemplary, and our family has loved our time with you. Kenny Rogers of Bonaire Baptist Church, your belief in the missional nature of our military and your willingness to come alongside our community has restored much hope for us in the local church. Last, Adam Bennett of Back Bay Church, thank you for giving us a place to crash and shepherding us well. The radical hospitality and life-giving compassion at Back Bay Church offered our family unbelievable restoration during the throes of deployment.

To Carol Kent: Saying "thank you" doesn't even begin to express the deep and abiding gratitude I have for you or for your willingness to partner with us in the advance of Christ's kingdom here on earth. You caught the vision of a mission-minded military community. With your invaluable investment in me as a leader, and with your encouragement for a generation of military spouse ministers, leaders, and freethinkers, you have launched a movement that I believe will change the world. Thank you for your wisdom, your servant's heart, your obedience to God in shepherding the Speak Up Conference, and for pointing us always back to Jesus.

To My Closest Crew: Katie Byrd, I can see God's handwriting in the DNA of our friendship. From the very start, your companionship has been an edifying and encouraging gift from our Father. Thank you for being my mirror, holding me accountable and exhorting me to holiness. Catherine Wehrman, your radical hospitality and the immense depth of your compassion have permanently changed me. Thank you for your extreme authenticity, heart to serve, and your supernatural ability to listen. Laura Early, the ferocity with which you serve others is awe-inspiring. Your giftedness has altered the course of this ministry in ways that are difficult to express. I am forever grateful for your heart for the Lord, your discernment of truth, and your guidance in leading. Andi Adams, the Holy Spirit in me recognizes the life of the Spirit in you. Your love for God, and your heart's desire to walk closely with His Spirit, has built my faith. I believe that your encouragement in the Spirit for leaders like me will impact generations to come. Jessica Manfre, I could not imagine a more perfect person to share this writing journey with. It is time to buckle up, light the flame, and ride the wave!

NOTES

WEEK ONE: SUMMONED TO THE START

1. Bible Hub, s.v. "exartizó," https://biblehub.com/greek/1822.htm.

2. You can easily find a map of the Persian Empire online, or you might have a Bible that includes maps. In addition, several fine atlases of the lands in the Bible are available.

3. Warren Wiersbe, *Be Committed* (Colorado Springs: David C. Cook, 1993), 84, quoting Herodotus, *The History, Book VII,* section 8.

4. Mayo Clinic, "Narcissistic Personality Disorder," https://www.mayoclinic.org/diseases-conditions/narcissistic-personality-disorder/symptoms-causes/syc-20366662.

5. Francis Bacon lived from 1561–1626. His *Essays* was first published in 1597; more essays were added to the second edition of 1612, and in 1625 another version with fifty-eight essays appeared. "On Revenge" is dated 1625.

6. Sarah Sumner, *Men and Women in the Church* (Downers Grove, IL: InterVarsity Press, 2003), 161–63.

WEEK TWO: SUMMONED TO SEEK

1. Karen H. Jobes, *Esther: The NIV Application Commentary* (Grand Rapids: Zondervan, 1999), 95.

2. You can read more about these events at GotQuestions.org: https://www.gotquestions.org/Babylonian-captivity-exile.html.

3. Karen H. Jobes, *Esther*, 99.

4. Bible Hub, s.v. "tamruq," https://biblehub.com/hebrew/8562.htm.

5. Rachel Friedlander, "Five Things about Esther That Nobody Talks About," Jews for Jesus, February 19, 2019, https://jewsforjesus.org/publications/issues/issues-v22-n09/five-things-about-esther-that-nobody-talks-about.

6. Michael G. Wechsler, "Esther," in *The Moody Bible Commentary*, Michael Rydelnik and Michael Vanlaningham, gen. eds. (Chicago: Moody, 2014), 687.

WEEK THREE: SUMMONED TO SCRUTINIZE

1. Another interpretation of the term Agagite is not that Haman was a descendant of the Amalekites but that the term is derogatory. Michael Wechsler, writing in the *Moody Bible Commentary*, adds, "Most likely, however, the term Agagite refers to Haman's origin in a certain region of Persia or Media, that is the district of Agag." *The Moody Bible Commentary*, Michael Rydelnik and Michael Vanlaningham, gen. eds. (Chicago: Moody, 2014), 687.

2. Blue Letter Bible, s.v. "chemah," https://www.blueletterbible.org/lang/lexicon/lexiconcfm?t=kjv&strongs=h2534.

3. Bible Hub, s.v. "goral," https://biblehub.com/hebrew/1486.htm.

4. Casting lots is mentioned dozens of times in the Old Testament and several times in the New Testament. This practice was one way God made His will known to His people. As Proverbs 16:33 points out, the people may toss the object, but the outcome is the Lord's decision. See https://www.gotquestions.org/casting-lots.html for an interesting discussion of this practice in Bible times.

5. Karen H. Jobes, *Esther: The NIV Application Commentary* (Grand Rapids: Zondervan, 1999), 121.

6. Latisha Morrison, *Be the Bridge: Pursuing God's Heart for Racial Reconciliation* (Colorado Springs: Waterbrook, 2019).

7. Ibid., 28.

8. You can find the Heidelberg Catechism from different sources with some variety in wording. The version quoted here is from *Ecumenical Creeds and Reformed Confessions* © 1988 Faith Alive Christian Resources, http://www.faithaliveresources.org. For an interesting exploration of this catechism and what it means for a contemporary Christian, see *The Good News We Almost Forgot: Rediscovering the Gospel in a 16th Century Catechism* by Kevin DeYoung (Chicago: Moody, 2010).

9. Interestingly, this Hebrew word is only used in two other places in the Old Testament: Exodus 14:3 and Joel 1:18.

10. Sara Barratt, quoted in Megan Brown, "'Love Riot' by Sara Barrett Calls Teenagers to Radical Love," *Military Spouse*, https://www.militaryspouse.com/military-life/love-riot-by-sara-barrett/.

WEEK FOUR: SUMMONED TO SHARE SORROW

1. *Merriam-Webster*, s.v. "lament," last updated January 31, 2021, https://www.merriam-webster.com/dictionary/lament.

2. J. D. Douglas and Merrill C. Tenney, *Zondervan Illustrated Bible Dictionary* (Zondervan: Grand Rapids, 1987), 128.

3. "Are God's Providence and God's Sovereignty the Same?," transcript of interview with John Piper, *Ask Pastor John*, Desiring God, October 18, 2019, https://www.desiringgod.org/interviews/are-gods-providence-and-gods-sovereignty-the-same.

4. Walter C. Kaiser Jr., *Preaching and Teaching from the Old Testament: A Guide for the Church* (Grand Rapids: Baker Academic, 2003), 125–26.

5. Karen H. Jobes, *Esther: The NIV Application Commentary* (Grand Rapids: Zondervan, 1999), 118.

6. A. W. Tozer, *A. W. Tozer: Three Spiritual Classics in One Volume* (Chicago: Moody, 2018), 190.

WEEK FIVE: SUMMONED TO SELFLESSNESS

1. David Strain, *Ruth & Esther: There Is a Redeemer and Sudden Reversals* (Ross-shire, UK: Christian Focus, 2018), 123.

2. Blue Letter Bible, s.v. "chen," https://www.blueletterbible.org/lang/lexicon/lexicon.cfm?t=kjv&strongs=h2580.

3. The phrase "half my kingdom" was an idiom that meant the "petitioner has gained great favor in the eyes of the king." *The Baker Illustrated Bible Commentary*, Gary M. Burge and Andrew E. Hill, eds. (Grand Rapids: Baker, 2012), 446.

4. C. S. Lewis, *Mere Christianity* (New York: MacMillan, 1943, 1945, 1952), 121.

5. Landon Dowden, *Exalting Jesus in Esther*, Christ-Centered Exposition Commentary (Nashville: Holman Reference, 2019), 136.

WEEK SIX: SUMMONED TO STUDY

1. John MacArthur, *Ruth & Esther: Women of Faith, Bravery, and Hope* (Nashville: W Publishing Group, 2000), 93.

2. Iain Duguid, *Esther & Ruth,* Reformed Expository Commentary (Phillipsburg, NJ: P&R Publishing, 2005) 96.

3. Patricia Kime, "In a First, Pentagon Releases Data on Military Spouse and Child Suicides," Military.com, September 27, 2019, https://www.military.com/daily-news/2019/09/27/first-pentagon-releases-data-military-spouse-and-child-suicides.html.

4. Refer to Week Four note 2 for information about the exile to Babylon.

5. Karen H. Jobes, *Esther: The NIV Application Commentary* (Grand Rapids: Zondervan, 1999), 178.

6. Michael G. Wechsler, "Esther," in *The Moody Bible Commentary*, Michael Rydelnik and Michael Vanlaningham, gen. eds. (Chicago: Moody, 2014), 691.

WEEK SEVEN: SUMMONED TO SIFT THE SCRIPTURES

1. Karen H. Jobes, *Esther: The NIV Application Commentary* (Grand Rapids: Zondervan, 1999), 188.

2. An excellent study on this topic is *7 Feasts: Finding Christ in the Sacred Celebrations of the Old Testament* by Erin Davis (Chicago: Moody, 2020).

WEEK EIGHT: SUMMONED TO SERVE

1. "Mary and Eve" by Sister Grace Remington, OCSO. Copyright to Our Lady of the Mississippi Abbey in Dubuque, Iowa. For more information about buying this as a print or Christmas cards, visit https://www.monasterycandy.com/Product_List?c=33.

2. Michael G. Wechsler, "Esther," in *The Moody Bible Commentary*, Michael Rydelnik and Michael Vanlaningham, gen. eds. (Chicago: Moody, 2014), 689.

3. For practical ways to share the good news of Christ, see *Sent: Living a Life That Invites Others to Jesus* by Heather Holleman and Ashley Holleman (Chicago: Moody, 2020).

Bible Studies for Women

IN-DEPTH. CHRIST-CENTERED. REAL IMPACT.

7 FEASTS
978-0-8024-1955-2

**AN UNEXPLAINABLE
LIFE**
978-0-8024-1473-1

**THE UNEXPLAINABLE
CHURCH**
978-0-8024-1742-8

**UNEXPLAINABLE
JESUS**
978-0-8024-1909-5

THIS I KNOW
978-0-8024-1596-7

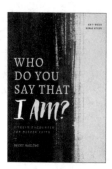

**WHO DO YOU SAY
THAT I AM?**
978-0-8024-1550-9

HE IS ENOUGH
978-0-8024-1686-5

KEEPING THE FAITH
978-0-8024-1931-6

Explore our Bible studies at
moodypublisherswomen.com

Also available as eBooks

MOODY PUBLISHERS
WOMEN
BIBLE STUDIES

Bible Studies for Women

IN-DEPTH. CHRIST-CENTERED. REAL IMPACT.

IF GOD IS FOR US
978-0-8024-1713-8

ON BENDED KNEE
978-0-8024-1919-4

HIS LAST WORDS
978-0-8024-1467-0

I AM FOUND
978-0-8024-1468-7

INCLUDED IN CHRIST
978-0-8024-1591-2

THE WAY HOME
978-0-8024-1983-5

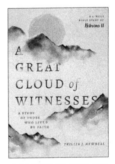

A GREAT CLOUD OF WITNESSES
978-0-8024-2107-4

HABAKKUK
978-0-8024-1980-4

Explore our Bible studies at
moodypublisherswomen.com
Also available as eBooks

MOODY PUBLISHERS
WOMEN
BIBLE STUDIES